Advanced SAS

Interview Questions

You'll Most Likely Be Asked

Job Interview Questions Series

 **Vibrant Publishers**

www.vibrantpublishers.com

Advanced SAS Interview Questions
You'll Most Likely Be Asked

ISBN-10: 1477500197
ISBN-13: 9781477500194

Library of Congress Control Number: 2012909254

This publication is designed to provide accurate and authoritative information in regard to the subject matter covered. The author has made every effort in the preparation of this book to ensure the accuracy of the information. However, information in this book is sold without warranty either expressed or implied. The Author or the Publisher will not be liable for any damages caused or alleged to be caused either directly or indirectly by this book.

Vibrant Publishers books are available at special quantity discount for sales promotions, or for use in corporate training programs. For more information please write to **bulkorders@vibrantpublishers.com**

Please email feedback / corrections (technical, grammatical or spelling) to **spellerrors@vibrantpublishers.com**

To access the complete catalogue of Vibrant Publishers, visit **www.vibrantpublishers.com**

Table of Contents

This page is intentionally left blank

Advanced SAS

Interview Questions

Review these typical interview questions and think about how you would answer them. Read the answers listed; you will find best possible answers along with strategies and suggestions.

This page is intentionally left blank

PROC SQL

1: How PROC SQL differs from other PROC statements in SAS?
Answer:

PROC SQL is unique and it differs from other SAS Procedures in the following ways:

a) Almost all the SAS procedures require RUN statement while PROC SQL does not require a RUN statement. PROC SQL executes each query automatically.

b) Unlike other SAS procedures the PROC SQL continues to run after you submit the step, so it is always necessary to submit a PROC step, DATA step or a QUIT statement to end the procedure.

c) Also PROC SQL has several statements which include clauses. This makes it unique compared to other SAS Procedures.

E.g.: The following program contains three statements - PROC SQL statement, SELECT statement and QUIT statement. The SELECT statement contains *select* clause, *from* clause, *where* clause and *order by* clause.

```
proc sql;
select type, slno, author
     from exam.questionset1
     where slno <30000
     order by type;
quit;
```

2: Suppose you are generating a report from the data set exam.questionset1 using PROC SQL. You wish to display the name of the column "author" as "writer" in the report. How do you write the query to modify the report?
Answer:

The following program generates a report from exam.questionset1 using PROC SQL. The column named *author* is assigned an alias *writer* in the report using the keyword AS. Column alias will appear as column heading in the output.

```
proc sql;
select type, slno, author as writer
```

    from exam.questionset1;
quit;

3: While generating a report using PROC SQL, how do you sort the rows in descending order of any particular column?
Answer:
The *order by* clause is used in the SELECT statement of PROC SQL to sort the rows in the output according to the values of a particular column. By default, *order by* clause sorts the rows in the ascending order. The rows can be sorted in the descending order of any column by specifying the keyword, *desc*, after the column name.
E.g.: The following program selects *type, slno* and *author* for all the rows having *slno* less than 30000. In the output, the rows are sorted according to the descending values of *slno*.
proc sql;
select type, slno, author
    from exam.questionset1
    where slno <30000
    order by slno desc;
quit;

4: What is referred to as "qualifying a column name"?
Answer:
"Qualifying a column name" refers to the process of prefixing the SAS data set name to a column name. This is done mostly in those situations where you need to select the data from two data sets and the two data sets have the same named columns. If you want to include one of the same named columns then you will have to prefix the name of the data set from which you wish to take the column to the column name in the query.
E.g.: The following PROC SQL query joins two data sets exam.set1 and exam.set2. Both the data sets contain the same column *slno*. So, to indicate the data set from which the value of *slno* is to be read, the name of the data set is prefixed to the column name in the *select* clause. This is referred to as "qualifying the column

name".

```
proc sql;
select type, set1.slno,author
    from exam.set1, exam.set2
    where set1.slno=set2.slno
    order by slno;
quit;
```

5: Is there any way to display all the column names from a data set without mentioning the names of the columns?

Answer:

Yes, an asterisk(*) can be used in the *select* clause to display all the columns in a data set.

E.g.: The following program selects all the columns from the data set exam.questionset1.

```
proc sql;
select *
    from exam.questionset1
quit;
```

6: What is the significance of FEEDBACK option?

Answer:

The FEEDBACK option is a debugging tool which helps us to see what is being submitted to the processor. When asterisk(*) is used with *select* clause, FEEDBACK option is used in the PROC SQL statement, which in turn writes the list of column names to SAS log.

E.g.: In the following program FEEDBACK option is used in the PROC SQL statement. This causes a detailed list of column names (*type, slno* and *author*) to be written to SAS log.

```
proc sql feedback;
select *
    from exam.questionset1
quit;
```

7: While using PROC SQL, how do you limit the number of

rows which is displayed in the output?

Answer:

The OUTOBS= option can be used in the PROC SQL statement to limit the number of rows displayed. OUTOBS= option is similar to OBS= data set option.

E.g.: The following program selects *type, slno* and *author* for all the rows having *slno* less than 30000. In the output, the rows are sorted according to the descending values of *slno*. Only 10 rows are displayed in the output as OUTOBS=10 is added to the PROC SQL statement.

```
proc sql outobs=10;
select type, slno, author
    from exam.questionset1
    where slno <30000
    order by slno desc;
quit;
```

8: Which keyword is used to eliminate the rows containing duplicate values while using PROC SQL?

Answer:

The DISTINCT keyword can be used in the SELECT statement to remove the rows that contain duplicate values. The DISTINCT keyword applies to all the columns mentioned in the SELECT statement.

E.g.: The following program selects *type, slno* and *author* from the data set exam.questionset1. Use of DISTINCT keyword removes the rows containing duplicate values.

```
proc sql ;
select distinct type, slno, author
    from exam.questionset1
    order by slno;
quit;
```

9: Explain BETWEEN-AND operator with example.

Answer:

The BETWEEN-AND operator is used to select rows based on a

range of numeric or character values.

E.g.: The following program displays all the rows whose *slno* is between 3000 and 4000.

```
proc sql ;
select *
    from exam.questionset1
    where slno between 3000 and 4000;
quit;
```

10: Explain the significance of CONTAINS operator.
Answer:

The CONTAINS operator is used to select the rows in which a character column includes a particular string.

E.g.: The following program displays all the rows in which *type* column contains the string 'tech'.

```
proc sql ;
select *
    from exam.questionset1
    where type contains 'tech';
quit;
```

11: How does IN operator function when used with PROC SQL?
Answer:

The IN operator is used to select those rows which match with one value among a fixed list of values. The fixed list can contain either numeric or character values. The list of values is enclosed in parenthesis.

E.g.: The following program displays all the rows for which *type* column contains the string 'technical' or 'fiction' or 'literature'. Also the character values in the list are enclosed in quotation marks.

```
proc sql ;
select *
    from exam.questionset1
    where type in ('technical', 'fiction', 'literature');
quit;
```

12: Which operator is used with PROC SQL to retrieve those rows for which a particular column has missing values?
Answer:
The IS MISSING operator can be used to select the rows for which particular column has missing values.
E.g.: Suppose you need to check if there are any rows for which the column *type* contains missing values then the following program can be used. This displays all the rows for which the *type* column contains missing values.
proc sql ;
select *
   from exam.questionset1
   where type is missing;
quit;

13: Is there any other operator which can be used in the place of IS MISSING operator?
Answer:
The IS NULL operator can be used to select the rows for which particular column has missing values. So IS NULL operator also can be used in the place of IS MISSING operator.
E.g.: Suppose you need to check if there are any rows for which the column *type* contains missing values then the following program can be used. This displays all the rows for which the *type* column contains missing values.
proc sql ;
select *
   from exam.questionset1
   where type is null;
quit;

Also if you know the data type of a column, you can use a comparison operator to check for the rows which contain missing values.
E.g.: The following program also selects those rows for which the *type* column contains missing values. Since *type* is a character

column, a blank is used in the quotation to represent the missing values.

```
proc sql ;
select *
    from exam.questionset1
    where type = ' ' ;
quit;
```

14: Explain the purpose of using the wild card operator underscore (_) with LIKE operator in PROC SQL.

Answer:

The LIKE operator is used to select the rows which have values that match with specific pattern of characters. The wild card operator underscore (_) is used to represent a single character value.

E.g.: The following program returns all those rows, whose *author* column contains values which start with T, end with M and which have a character in between. This program will return rows in which *author* column contains values like Tom, Tim, Tam etc.

```
proc sql ;
select *
    from exam.questionset1
    where author like 'T_m';
quit;
```

15: Explain the purpose of using the wild card operator percent (%) with LIKE operator in PROC SQL.

Answer:

The LIKE operator is used to select the rows which have values that match with specific pattern of characters. The wild card operator percent (%) is used to represent any number of character values.

E.g.: The following program returns all those rows, whose *city* column contains values which start with S, end with E and which have any number of characters in between. This program will return rows in which *city* column contains values like Sunnyvale,

Susanville, Springville, Sanjose etc.

proc sql ;
select *
    from exam.questionset1
    where city like 'S%e';
quit;

16: Explain the functionality of SOUNDS-LIKE (=*) operator.

Answer:
The SOUNDS-LIKE (=*) operator is used to select the rows which have values that sound like another value you specify. The SOUNDS-LIKE operator uses soundex algorithm to compare the values of a column with the words specified.
E.g.: The following program returns all those rows, whose *author* column contains values that sound like *Justin*. This query returns the rows whose *author* column contains values like *Justin, Jestin, Jesstin* etc.

proc sql ;
select *
    from exam.questionset1
    where author =* 'Justin';
quit;

17: Is it possible to define a new column after performing a calculation using SELECT clause?
Answer:
Yes, it is possible to define a new column after performing a calculation in *select* clause.
E.g.: The following program selects *type, slno* from the data set exam.questionset1. This also creates a new column, marks, by taking the sum of three columns, *marksphy, markschem* and *marksbio*.

proc sql ;
select type, slno, marksphy+markschem+marksbio as marks,
    from exam.questionset1;
quit;

18: How do you reference a column in the WHERE clause, whose value is calculated in the SELECT clause of the same PROC SQL query?

Answer:

While using those columns in the *where* clause whose values are computed in the *select* clause of the same PROC SQL query, it is always necessary to specify the keyword CALCULATED. The absence of the keyword CALCULATED will generate an error message in the SAS log.

E.g.: The following program selects *type, slno* from the data set exam.questionset1. This also creates a new column, *marks*, by taking the sum of three columns, *marksphy, markschem* and *marksbio*. This displays those rows where the value of *marks* is greater than 80. Also while using the calculated column *marks* in the *where* clause , it is necessary to use the keyword CALCULATED.

```
proc sql ;
select type, slno, marksphy+markschem+marksbio as marks,
    from exam.questionset1
    where calculated marks > 80;
quit;
```

19: How do you specify a label for a column in the PROC SQL query?

Answer:

The data set options LABEL= can be used after the column name in the *select* clause to label the column. By default PROC SQL uses the labels which are already stored in the data set. The use of LABEL= option overrides the default label.

E.g.: The following program selects *type, slno* and *author* from the data set exam.questionset1. The LABEL= option has been used to specify the name of the column author as 'Writer'.

```
proc sql ;
select type, slno, author label = 'Writer'
    from exam.questionset1
    order by slno;
```

quit;

20: How do you specify a format for a calculated column in the PROC SQL query?

Answer:

The data set options FORMAT= can be used after the column name in the *select* clause to apply format for the column. By default PROC SQL uses the formats which are already stored in the data set for the columns present in the data set.

E.g.: The following program selects *type*, *slno* and *author* from the data set exam.questionset1. The *select* clause adds the values of the columns *marks1* and *marks2* to calculate the value of the column, *totalmarks*. The FORMAT= option has been used to specify the format of the column *totalmarks*.

```
proc sql ;
select type, slno, author , marks1+marks2 as totalmarks
format=comma5.2
    from exam.questionset1
    order by slno;
quit;
```

21: How do you specify a title statement with a PROC SQL query?

Answer:

While specifying the title statements with a PROC SQL query the title statements must be placed in either of the following locations:
    a) Before the PROC SQL statement
    b) Between the PROC SQL statement and *select* clause.
E.g.: In the following program a title is specified between PROC SQL statement and *select* clause.

```
proc sql ;
title 'Marks Details';
select type, slno, author , marks1+marks2 as totalmarks
format=comma5.2
    from exam.questionset1
    order by slno;
```

quit;

OR

In the following program a title is specified before PROC SQL statement.

```
title 'Marks Details';
proc sql ;
select type, slno, author , marks1+marks2 as totalmarks
format=comma5.2
    from exam.questionset1
    order by slno;
quit;
```

22: How do you add a column containing character constant to the output while using PROC SQL query?

Answer:

To add a column containing a character constant to output, you need to add the text string in quotation marks in the *select* clause. E.g.: The following program selects *type, slno* and *author* from the data set exam.questionset1. The *select* clause adds the values of the columns *marks1* and *marks2* to calculate the value of the column, *totalmarks*. The FORMAT= option has been used to specify the format of the column *totalmarks*. Here a text string 'Total marks is:' has been added in the *select* clause. So the output would contain an additional column between *author* and calculated column. The new column would have the value 'Total marks is:' for all the rows.

```
proc sql ;
select type,
    slno,
     author ,
    'Total marks is:',
     marks1+marks2 format=comma5.2
    from exam.questionset1
    order by slno;
```

quit;

23: How is a summary function processed when it has a single argument?

Answer:

When a summary function has a single argument, the calculation is performed down the column. Some functions like AVG, COUNT can be used only with one argument.

E.g.: The following program illustrates the use of a summary function (AVG) when it has a single argument. Here the PROC SQL query calculates the average of all the marks and it displays it as *Average marks*.

```
proc sql ;
select avg(marks) as Average marks
    from exam.questionset1;
quit;
```

24: Explain what happens when a summary function specifies multiple columns as arguments.

Answer:

When a summary function has multiple arguments, the calculation is performed across the columns for each row.

E.g.: The following program illustrates the use of a summary function (SUM) which has multiple arguments. Here the sum of the variables *marks1, marks2* and *marks3* is calculated for each row and it is displayed as *totalmarks*.

```
proc sql ;
select sum(marks1, marks2 , marks3) as totalmarks
    from exam.questionset1;
quit;
```

25: How does a PROC SQL process a summary function with a GROUP BY clause?

Answer:

When PROC SQL processes a summary function which has a GROUP BY clause in the same query, it applies the summary

function to each group specified in the GROUP BY clause.
E.g.: The following program illustrates the use of a summary
function (AVG). Here the summary function AVG is applied to
each group of the variable *type*.

proc sql ;
select type, avg(marks) as Average marks
    from exam.questionset1
group by type;
quit;

26: How does PROC SQL process a summary function without a GROUP BY clause?

Answer:

When PROC SQL processes a summary function without a
GROUP BY clause, it applies the summary function to the entire
data set.

E.g.: The following program illustrates the use of a summary
function (AVG). Here the summary function AVG is applied to
the entire data set. It calculates the average of the variable *marks*.

proc sql ;
select type, avg(marks) as Average marks
    from exam.questionset1;
quit;

27: How does PROC SQL calculate the output when SELECT clause has additional columns listed outside the summary function?

Answer:

When *select* clause of a PROC SQL contains columns listed outside
the summary functions, then it calculates the value of the function
for the entire data set if the GROUP BY clause is absent and if the
GROUP BY clause is present, it calculates the value for each
group. It displays all the rows of output with this value repeated.
E.g.: In the following program there are columns outside the
summary function in the *select* clause like the *type* column. Also
there is a GROUP BY clause, so the PROC SQL calculates the

value of *avg(marks)* for each group of the variable *type*. The output contains these values repeated for all the rows within each group.

```
proc sql ;
select type, avg(marks) as Average marks
    from exam.questionset1;
group by type;
quit;
```

28: How does PROC SQL calculate the output when SELECT clause has no additional columns listed outside the summary function?

Answer:

When *select* clause of a PROC SQL contains no columns listed outside the summary functions, then it calculates and displays a single value using the summary function for the entire data set if there is no GROUP BY clause. If there are no columns listed outside the summary function and if there is a GROUP BY clause then PROC SQL calculates the value for each group.

E.g.: In the following program there are no columns outside the summary function in the *select* clause. Also there is a GROUP BY clause, so the PROC SQL calculates the value of *avg(marks)* for each group of the variable *type*. So a single value is produced for each group.

```
proc sql ;
select avg(marks) as Average marks
    from exam.questionset1;
group by type;
quit;
```

29: Which function is used to calculate the total number of rows in a data set or a group?

Answer:

COUNT function can be used to calculate the total number of rows in a data set or a group.

E.g.: The following program calculates the total number of rows in the data set exam.questionset1. The variable *count* contains the

total number of rows in the data set.
proc sql ;
select count(*) as count
      from exam.questionset1;
quit;
The following program calculates the total number of rows in the
data set exam.questionset1 for each group of the variable *type*. The
variable count contains the total number of rows in the data set.
proc sql ;
select count(*) as count
      from exam.questionset1;
group by type
quit;

30: How do you use the COUNT function to calculate the non-missing values for a specific column rather than a data set?
Answer:
Suppose you wish to calculate the number of non-missing values
for a specific column instead of a data set, then COUNT function
can be used with specific column as an argument.
E.g.: The following program calculates the total number of non-missing values in the column *slno*. COUNT function always
ignores the missing values.
proc sql ;
select count(slno) as count
      from exam.questionset1;
quit;

31: How do you use the COUNT function to calculate the unique values for a specific column?
Answer:
Suppose you wish to calculate the number of unique values for a
specific column using COUNT function, then the keyword
DISTINCT needs to be added before the column name. The
keyword DISTINCT along with column name forms the argument
of the COUNT function.

E.g.: The following program calculates the number of unique values for the variable *type*.

```
proc sql ;
select count(distinct type) as count
    from exam.questionset1;
quit;
```

32: What is a subquery?
Answer:

A subquery is a query nested in another query. PROC SQL can contain subqueries upto one or more levels.

E.g.: In the following program, a subquery calculates the *avg(marks)* for the entire data set exam.questionset1 and returns to the outer query. The outer query displays the rows grouped by the variable *type*. The values are displayed for those groups whose *averagemarks* is greater than the *averagemarks* for the entire data set.

```
proc sql ;
select type, avg(marks) as averagemarks
    from exam.questionset1
    group by type
    having avg(marks)>
        (select avg(marks)
        from exam.questionset1;);
quit;
```

33: Explain a non correlated multiple value subquery used with conditional operator IN.
Answer:

A non correlated subquery is a subquery which executes independent of the outer query. That is the inner query does not require any values passed to it by the outer query. When the non correlated subquery returns more than one value it becomes non correlated multiple value subquery.

E.g.: The following program illustrates the concept of non correlated multiple value subquery used with conditional operator IN. Here the subquery selects the *slno* for all those rows where the value of *marks* is greater than 80. The subquery returns the values of all the selected *slno* to the outer query. The outer query displays the data *(type, author)* for the selected values of *slno*.

proc sql ;
select slno, type, author
    from exam.questionset1
    where slno in
        (select slno
        from exam.questionset1
        where marks>80);
quit;

34: Explain what happens when a non correlated multiple value subquery is used with outer query having operator ANY.

Answer:

A non correlated subquery can be used with the comparison operator ANY. When the outer query contains a comparison operator modified by ANY, then the outer query compares each value that it retrieves against the values returned by the subquery. All the values for which the comparison is TRUE are included in the output. Use of ANY causes this comparison to be TRUE if the comparison becomes TRUE for any one of the values returned by the subquery.

E.g.: The following program illustrates the concept of non correlated multiple value subquery used with operator ANY. Here the subquery selects marks for all those rows where the values of *type* are technical i.e. all subqueries return the value of all marks which fall into the technical category. The outer query displays the data *(type, author, slno* and *marks)* for nontechnical category whose value of *marks* is greater than any of the values returned by the subquery. So the output displays only those rows which fall in the nontechnical *type* and which have *marks* greater than any *marks* returned by the subquery.

proc sql ;
select slno, type, author, marks

from exam.questionset1
where

type= 'nontechnical' and
marks > any
        (select marks
        from exam.questionset1
        where type= 'technical');
quit;

35: Explain what happens when a non correlated multiple value subquery is used with outer query having operator ALL.
Answer:
A non correlated subquery can be used with the comparison operator ALL. When the outer query contains a comparison operator modified by ALL, then the outer query compares each value which it retrieves against the values returned by the subquery. All the values for which the comparison is TRUE are included in the output. Use of ALL causes this comparison to be TRUE if the comparison becomes TRUE for all of the values returned by the subquery.
E.g.: The following program illustrates the concept of non correlated multiple value subquery used with operator ALL. Here the subquery selects marks for all those rows where the values of *type* are technical i.e. all subqueries return the value of all *marks* which fall into the technical category. The outer query displays the data *(type, author, slno* and *marks)* for nontechnical category whose value of *marks* is greater than all values returned by the subquery. So the output displays only those rows which fall in the nontechnical *type* and which have marks greater than all the *marks* in the technical category.
proc sql ;
select slno, type, author, marks
        from exam.questionset1
        where

type= 'nontechnical' and
marks > all
    (select marks
    from exam.questionset1
    where type= 'technical');
quit;

36: Explain operator EXISTS with example.

Answer:

EXISTS is a conditional operator which is used to check for the
existence of values returned by the subquery.

E.g.: Suppose you have two data sets - exam.invigilators, which
contains the information (name, ID, institution) about the
invigilators and exam.schedule, which contains one row that is
assigned to each invigilator who is assigned to duty for each date.
ID is the column common in both the data sets and each
invigilator has a unique ID. So while considering both the data
sets, common part would be those invigilators who have been
assigned the duty. To find the result the following query can be
used. The subquery selects all those rows from exam.schedule
where the values of *invigilators.id* and *schedule.id* match. The
conditional operator EXISTS works in such a way that this
condition becomes TRUE if the subquery returns atleast one row.
If the condition is TRUE then the outer query selects *name, id,* and
institution from exam.invigilators.

proc sql ;
select name, ID, Institution
    from exam.invigilators
    where exists
        (select *
        from exam.schedule
        where invigilators.id= schedule.id);
quit;

37: In PROC SQL how do you verify the syntax of the query without executing it?

Answer:
NOEXEC option can be used in the PROC SQL statement to verify the syntax of the query without executing it.
E.g.: In the following program NOEXEC option is used to check the syntax of the query. If the query is valid and all the referenced columns exist then a message is written to SAS log stating that *SAS statement not executed due to noexec option* which indicates that syntax is correct. If there is any error in syntax or column does not exist then an error message is written to SAS log. Thus it is possible to verify the syntax without executing a query.
proc sql noexec ;
select slno, type , author
      from exam.questionset1
      where slno between 3000 and 4000;
quit;

38: Explain the VALIDATE keyword.
Answer:
VALIDATE keyword can also be used in the PROC SQL statement to verify the syntax of the query without executing it. VALIDATE statement does not require a semi-colon and it is specified after PROC SQL statement but before *select* clause.
E.g.: In the following program VALIDATE keyword is used to check the syntax of the query. If the query is valid and all the referenced columns exist then a message is written to SAS log stating that *PROC SQL statement has valid syntax.* If there is any error in syntax or column does not exist then an error message is written to SAS log.
proc sql;
validate
select slno, type , author
      from exam.questionset1
where slno between 3000 and 4000;
quit;

39: What is the main difference between NOEXEC option and

VALIDATE keyword?

Answer:

The major difference between NOEXEC option and VALIDATE keyword is that VALIDATE keyword is applicable only to the SELECT statement following it whereas NOEXEC option is applicable to all the queries in the PROC SQL step.

Horizontal Joins

40: What is a Cartesian product?

Answer:

PROC SQL helps in combining the data from different data sets and joining the data. During the process of joining various data sets, SAS begins by generating *Cartesian product*. *Cartesian product* contains all possible combinations of rows from different data sets.

E.g.: In the following program, two data sets – exam.questionset1 and exam.questionset2 are included in the *from* clause and there is no *where* clause. So it returns *Cartesian product*. *Cartesian product* contains all possible combinations of rows from both the data sets. First row of the data set, exam.questionset1, is combined with each row of exam.questionset2. Then second row of exam.questionset1 is combined with each row of exam.questionset2 and so on. The *Cartesian product* contains all the possible combination of rows from the input data sets and all the columns. Columns with same names are displayed separately.

```
proc sql;
select *
    from exam.questionset1, exam.questionset2;
quit;
```

41: Explain inner join with examples.

Answer:

Inner join is a type of join which displays only those rows from the first data set which match with rows in the second data set based on the criteria specified in the *where* clause.

E.g.: In the following program, two data sets – exam.set1 and exam.set2 are combined using an inner join. So the output contains only those rows whose value of column *slno* in exam.set1 is equal to the value of *slno* in exam.set2.

```
proc sql;
select *
    from exam.set1, exam.set2
    where set1.slno=set2.slno ;
quit;
```

42: What is the maximum number of tables which can be specified in a single inner join?

Answer:

It is possible to combine a maximum of 32 tables in a single inner join.

43: While using inner join, is it possible to specify columns with different names in the join condition?

Answer:

Yes, it is possible to specify columns with different names in the join condition of an inner join. But PROC SQL will process an inner join only if the columns specified are of same data type. E.g.: In the following program, two data sets – exam.set1 and exam.set2 are combined using an inner join. So the output contains only those rows whose value of column *slno* in exam.set1 is equal to the value of *id* in exam.set2. The column names specified in the join condition are different (*slno* and *id*) but they are of the same data type.

```
proc sql;
select *
     from exam.set1, exam.set2
     where set1.slno=set2.id ;
quit;
```

44: Is column alias allowed while writing a query for inner join of two data sets?

Answer:

Yes, the column aliases are allowed while writing a query for inner join of two data sets.

E.g.: In the following program, two data sets – exam.set1 and exam.set2 are combined using an inner join. So the output contains only those rows whose value of column *slno* in exam.set1 is equal to the value of *id* in exam.set2. Also the column *slno* from the data set exam.set1 has been renamed to *order*. So the alias order is displayed in the *output*.

```
proc sql;
```

```
select set1.slno as order , type, author, set2.id
    from exam.set1, exam.set2
    where set1.slno=set2.id ;
quit;
```

45: How do you specify an alias for a data set in inner join?
Answer:
The alias for a data set is optional and is specified in the *from* clause on a PROC SQL query. It is helpful in those cases where the name of data set is quite lengthy.

E.g.: In the following program, two data sets – exam.questionset1 and exam.questionset2 are combined using an inner join. In the *from* clause an alias *s1* has been specified for the data set exam.questionset1 and an alias *s2* has been specified for the data set exam.questionset2. This alias is used in the *where* condition. The alias is very helpful as it helps in avoiding the writing of lengthy data set names.

```
proc sql;
select *
    from exam.questionset1 as s1,
    exam.questionset2 as s2
where s1.slno=s2.id ;
quit;
```

46: When does an alias for a data set become essential?
Answer:
Mentioning an alias for a data set becomes essential under the following conditions:

a) When a data set is joined to itself. This is also referred to as self join.

E.g.: In the following program, the same data set – exam.questionset1 is combined to itself using an inner join. In the *from* clause, alias *s1, s2* have been specified for the data set exam.questionset1.

```
proc sql;
    select *
```

```
        from exam.questionset1 as s1,
             exam.questionset1 as s2
    where s1.slno=s2.id ;
    quit;
```

b) When you need to reference the columns from data sets
    which have the same name but are in different libraries.
    E.g.: In the following program, two data sets –
    exam.questionset1 and result.questionset1 are combined
    using an inner join. In the *from* clause an alias *s1* has been
    specified for the data set exam.questionset1 and an alias *s2*
    has been specified for the data set result.questionset1. This
    alias is used in the *where* condition. Since the data sets are
    having the same name, alias helps in avoiding the
    confusion.

```
    proc sql;
    select *
        from exam.questionset1 as s1,
             result.questionset1 as s2
        where s1.slno=s2.id ;
    quit;
```

47: Explain the left outer join with example.
Answer:
Left outer join is a type of join which displays all those rows from
the first data set that match with rows in the second data set based
on the criteria plus the non matching rows from the data set which
is mentioned first in the *from* clause.
E.g.: In the following program, two data sets – exam.set1 and
exam.set2 are combined using a left outer join. So the output
contains those rows whose value of column *slno* in exam.set1 is
equal to the value of *slno* in exam.set2 plus all the rows (which are
matching as well as non matching) from exam.set1.

```
proc sql;
select *
    from exam.set1
    left join
```

```
    exam.set2
    on set1.slno=set2.slno ;
quit;
```

48: Explain the right outer join with example.
Answer:
Right outer join is a type of join which displays all those rows from the first data set that match with rows in the second data set based on the criteria plus the non matching rows from the dataset which is mentioned second in the *from* clause.
E.g.: In the following program, two data sets – exam.set1 and exam.set2 are combined using a right outer join. So the output contains those rows whose value of column *slno* in exam.set1 is equal to the value of *slno* in exam.set2 plus all the rows (which are matching as well as non matching) from exam.set2.

```
proc sql;
select *
    from exam.set1
    right join
    exam.set2
    on set1.slno=set2.slno ;
quit;
```

49: What is a full outer join?
Answer:
Full outer join is a type of join which retrieves all the rows from both the data sets mentioned in the *from* clause. It retrieves matching as well non matching rows.
E.g.: In the following program, two data sets – exam.set1 and exam.set2 are combined using a full outer join. So the output contains all the rows of exam.set1 as well as all the rows of exam.set2.

```
proc sql;
select *
    from exam.set1
    full join
```

exam.set2
on set1.slno=set2.slno ;
quit;

50: Can an inner join be created using an outer join syntax? If so how many tables can be joined at a time?
Answer:
Yes, an inner join can be created with an outer join syntax. An inner join which uses this syntax can be performed only on two tables at a time.
E.g.: In the following program, two data sets – exam.set1 and exam.set2 are combined using an inner join. So the output contains those rows whose value of column *slno* in exam.set1 is equal to the value of *slno* in exam.set2.
proc sql;
select *
    from exam.set1
    inner join
exam.set2
on set1.slno=set2.slno ;
quit;

51: What is the difference between the technique of "data step match merging" and PROC SQL joins?
Answer:
The main difference between the "data step match merging" and PROC SQL join is that while performing joins it is not necessary to sort the data first. However, while doing data step match merging, it is essential to sort the data.

52: Suppose you wish to merge two data sets by a selected variable, which join will produce the same result as "match merging" when all the values of selected variables match?
Answer:
When all the values of the selected variables match, an INNER JOIN will produce the same result as "data step match merging".

E.g.: In the following program, two data sets – exam.set1 and exam.set2 are combined using an INNER JOIN. So the output contains those rows whose value of column *slno* in exam.set1 is equal to the value of *slno* in exam.set2.

```
proc sql;
select *
    from exam.set1
    inner join
    exam.set2
on set1.slno=set2.slno ;
order by slno;
quit;
```

The result which is produced by the above query is identical to the result produced by the following "data step match merge" when all the values of the variable *slno* match in both the data sets.

In the below program both the data sets are sorted by the variable *slno* then data step is used to merge both the data sets. *proc print* displays the report.

```
proc sort data= exam.set1;
by slno;
run;
proc sort data= exam.set2;
by slno;
run;
data exam.merge;
    merge exam.set1 exam.set2;
    by slno;
run;
proc print data=exam.merge;
run;
```

53: Explain the COALESCE function.
Answer:
COALESCE function is used to overlay two or more columns while performing an inner or outer join.

E.g.: In the following program, two data sets – exam.set1 and exam.set2 are combined using a FULL OUTER JOIN. The data set exam.set1 has the following columns – *slno* and *type*. The data set exam.set2 has the following columns – *slno* and *author*. So the output contains all the rows (matching as well as non matching) of both exam.set1 and exam.set2. Here the COALESCE function is used to overlay the column of same data type. Here the two columns *slno* of exam.set1 and *slno* of exam.set2 are overlaid to produce a single column, *finalslno*, in the output.

```
proc sql;
select coalesce(set1.slno , set2.slno) as finalslno, type, author
    from exam.set1
    full join
exam.set2
on set1.slno=set2.slno ;
order by slno;
quit;
```

54: Suppose you wish to merge two data sets by a selected variable, which join will produce the same result as "match merging" when only some of the values of selected variables match?

Answer:

When only some of the values of the selected variables match, a FULL OUTER JOIN will produce the same result as "data step match merging".

E.g.: In the following program, two data sets – exam.batch1 and result.batch2 are combined using a FULL OUTER JOIN. The data set exam.batch1 has the following columns - *id* and *weightage*. The data set result.batch2 has the following columns - *id* and *author*. So the output contains all the rows (matching as well as non matching) of both exam.batch1 and result.batch2. Here the COALESCE function is used to overlay the column of same data type. Here the two columns *id* of exam.batch1 and *id* of result.batch2 are overlaid to produce a single column in the output.

```
proc sql;
select coalesce(batch1.id , batch2.id) as UniqueID, weightage,
author
    from exam.batch1
    full join
result.batch2
on batch1.id=batch2.id ;
order by id;
quit;
```

The result which is produced by the above query is identical to the result produced by the following "data step match merge" when only some of the values of the variable *id* match in both the data sets.
In the below program both the data sets are sorted by the variable *id* then data step is used to merge both the data sets. *proc print* displays the report.

```
proc sort data= exam.batch1;
by id;
run;
proc sort data= result.batch2;
by id;
run;
data exam.merge;
    merge exam.batch1 result.batch2;
    by id;
run;
proc print data=exam.merge;
run;
```

55: Does PROC SQL allow any other comparison operator other than "equal to" sign?
Answer:
Yes, PROC SQL can use other comparison operators like "greater than" and "less than" operators.
E.g.: In the following program, two data sets – exam.set1 and

exam.set2 are combined using an inner join. So the output contains only those rows whose value of column *slno* in exam.set1 is equal to the value of *slno* in exam.set2 and the value of *marks* in set1 is greater than the value of *marks* in set2.

```
proc sql;
select *
    from exam.set1, exam.set2
    where set1.marks > set2.marks
    and set1.slno=set2.slno ;
quit;
```

56: What is an IN-LINE view?
Answer:
An IN-LINE view is a nested query which is nested in the *from* clause of an outer query. An in-line view selects data from one or more different tables to produce a temporary table which the outer query uses as the data source. In-line view reduces the complexity of the code as well as increases the efficiency.

E.g.: In the following program, the outer query selects the data from an in-line view. The in-line view selects the data from the data set exam.set2. The in-line view returns the *slno, type* and *marks* for all those rows whose value of the variable *marks* is greater than 80. The outer query formats the data and displays the output.

```
proc sql;
select slno label='ID',
    type label='Technical',
    marks
    from (select slno, type ,marks
        from exam.set2
        where set2.marks > 80);
quit;
```

57: Which clause cannot be used with an in-line view?
Answer:
An ORDER BY clause cannot be used with an in-line view as it

generates errors. The errors are written to SAS log along with a message indicating that the processing of PROC SQL step is stopped.

58: What is the scope of an in-line view?
Answer:
An in-line view exists only during a query execution. So it cannot be referenced outside the query in which it is defined. Also an alias can be assigned to an in-line view but it cannot be assigned a permanent name.

59: Is it possible to combine an in-line view with other data sets?
Answer:
Yes, it is possible to combine an in-line view with other data sets. A PROC SQL query can join multiple data sets and in-line views. E.g.: In the following program, the outer query selects the data from an in-line view and a data set exam.set1. The in-line view selects the data from the data set exam.set2 and the in-line view is assigned as alias s2. The in-line view returns the *slno*, *type* and *marks* for all those rows whose value of the variable *marks* is greater than 80. The outer query formats the data and displays the output for all those rows from the data set exam.set1 and the in-line view whose variable, *slno* is matching.

```
proc sql;
select s2.slno label='ID',
     type label='Technical',
     marks
         from exam.set1 as s1
             (select slno, type ,marks
                 from exam.set2
                     where set2.marks > 80) as s2
         where s1.slno=s2.slno;
quit;
```

60: In how many data sets can the outer join be performed at a time?

Answer:

An outer join can only be performed only on two data sets at a time.

61: Is it possible to include multiple data sets in an in-line view? If so how?

Answer:

Yes, it is possible to include multiple tables in an in-line view. E.g.: The following program illustrates an in-line query which references multiple data sets - exam.set1 and exam.set2. The in-line query selects those rows from the data sets whose values of the variables, *slno* and *date* match. The outer query formats the values and displays the output.

```
proc sql;
select slno,
    type label='technical questions'
    marks,
        from
        (select slno, type ,marks
            from exam.set2, exam.set3
                where set2.slno = set3.slno
                and set2.date=set3.date) ;
quit;
```

This page is intentionally left blank

Vertical Joins

62: Explain the significance of EXCEPT operator.

Answer:

EXCEPT operator is used to select unique rows from the first data set that are not present in the second data set. This is a very powerful operator which is used for performing vertical joins. E.g.: The following program shows the operation of an EXCEPT operator. The output of the following query would be all the unique rows from the data set exam.set1 which are not present in the data set exam.set2.

```
proc sql;
select *
    from exam.set1
except
select *
    from exam.set2;
quit;
```

63: How are columns overlaid while using an EXCEPT operator in a PROC SQL query?

Answer:

While using an EXCEPT operator with a PROC SQL query to vertically combine two data sets, the columns (variables) from the two data sets are combined based on their position in the *select* clause. When columns are overlaid, PROC SQL uses the column name from the first data set. It is required that the columns which are mentioned in the same relative position in both the *select* clauses should be of the same data type otherwise it will generate an error.

E.g.: The following program shows the operation of an EXCEPT operator. The output of the following query would be all the unique rows from the data set exam.set1 which are not present in the data set exam.set2. The output will contain two columns *slno* and *author*. In the output the value of the column name is taken from the first data set.

```
proc sql;
select slno, author
```

```
      from exam.set1
except
select id, author
      from exam.set2;
quit;
```

64: Which keyword can be used with EXCEPT operator to select unique as well as duplicate rows from the first data set?

Answer:

The keyword ALL can be used with EXCEPT operator to select all the rows (both unique and duplicate) from the first data set which are not present in the second data set.

E.g.: The following program shows the operation of an EXCEPT operator along with the keyword ALL. The output of the following query would be all the rows (both unique as well as duplicate) from the data set exam.set1 which are not present in the data set exam.set2.

```
proc sql;
select *
      from exam.set1
except all
select *
      from exam.set2;
quit;
```

65: Explain the significance of CORR keyword while used with EXCEPT operator.

Answer:

The keyword CORR is used with EXCEPT operator to select only those variables / columns which have the same name. Here the output will have all those unique rows which are present in first data set which are not present in the second data set.

E.g.: The following program shows the operation of an EXCEPT operator with the keyword CORR. The output of the following query would be the unique rows from the data set exam.set1 which are not present in the data set exam.set2. Also the output has only one column, *author*, since only that column has same name in both the data sets.

```
proc sql;
select slno, author
    from exam.set1
except corr
select id, author
    from exam.set2;
quit;
```

66: What happens when both the keywords ALL and CORR are used with EXCEPT operator at a time?

Answer:

When the keywords ALL and CORR are used with EXCEPT operator at a time, all the rows (both unique and duplicate) will get displayed which are in the first data set and which are not in the second data set. Only those columns with same name are displayed in the output.

E.g.: The following program shows the operation of an EXCEPT operator with the keywords CORR and ALL. The output of the following query would be all those rows (both unique and duplicate) from the data set exam.set1 which are not present in the data set exam.set2. Also the output has only one column, *author*, since only that column has same name in both the data sets.

```
proc sql;
select slno, author
    from exam.set1
except corr all
select id, author
    from exam.set2;
quit;
```

67: Explain the significance of INTERSECT operator.

Answer:

INTERSECT operator is used to select unique rows which are common in both the data sets. INTERSECT operator also overlays

the columns based on the position in the *select* clause.
E.g.: The following program shows the operation of an
INTERSECT operator. The output of the following query would
be all unique rows which are common in both the data sets
exam.set1 and exam.set2. The columns will be overlaid and the
result will have the column names from the first data set
exam.set1.

```
proc sql;
select *
     from exam.set1
intersect
select *
     from exam.set2;
quit;
```

68: How do the keywords ALL and CORR affect the results when used with INTERSECT operator?

Answer:

The keyword ALL when used with INTERSECT operator, selects
all the rows (both unique and duplicate) which are common in
both the data sets.
E.g.: The following program shows the operation of an
INTERSECT operator with the keyword ALL. The output of the
following query would be all the rows (both unique as well as
duplicate) which are common in both the data sets exam.set1 and
exam.set2.

```
proc sql;
select *
     from exam.set1
intersect all
select *
     from exam.set2;
quit;
```

The keyword CORR when used with INTERSECT operator helps
to select rows based on the column name and not column

position. The result has those unique rows which are common in both the data sets.

E.g.: The following program shows the operation of an INTERSECT operator with the keyword CORR. The output of the following query would be the unique common rows from both the data sets exam.set1 and exam.set2. Also the output has only one column, *author*, since only that column has same name in both the data sets.

```
proc sql;
select slno, author
      from exam.set1
intersect corr
select id, author
      from exam.set2;
quit;
```

When the keywords ALL and CORR are used with INTERSECT operator at a time, all the rows (both unique and duplicate) will get displayed which are common in the both the data sets. Only those columns with the same name are displayed in the output. E.g.: The following program shows the operation of an INTERSECT operator with the keywords CORR and ALL. The output of the following query would be all those rows (both unique and duplicate) which are common in both the data sets exam.set1 and exam.set2. Also the output has only one column, *author*, since only that column has same name in both the data sets.

```
proc sql;
select slno, author
      from exam.set1
intersect corr all
select id, author
      from exam.set2;
quit;
```

69: Explain the significance of UNION operator.

Answer:
UNION operator is used to select those rows which are unique in a combined set of rows from both the data sets. UNION operator also overlays the columns based on the position in the *select* clause.
E.g.: The following program shows the operation of an UNION operator. The output of the following query would be all the unique rows from both the data sets exam.set1 and exam.set2. The columns will be overlaid and the result will have the column names from the first data set exam.set1.

```
proc sql;
select *
    from exam.set1
union
select *
    from exam.set2;
quit;
```

70: How do the keywords ALL and CORR affect the results when used with UNION operator?
Answer:
The keyword ALL when used with UNION operator, selects all the rows (both unique and duplicate) from the combined set of rows taken from both the data sets.
E.g.: The following program shows the operation of an UNION operator with the keyword ALL. The output of the following query would be all the rows (both unique as well as duplicate) from the data sets exam.set1 and exam.set2.

```
proc sql;
select *
    from exam.set1
union all
select *
    from exam.set2;
quit;
```

The keyword CORR when used with UNION operator helps to select rows based on the column name and not column position. The result has those unique rows from both the data sets. E.g.: The following program shows the operation of an UNION operator with the keyword CORR. The output of the following query would be the unique rows from both the data sets exam.set1 and exam.set2. Also the output has only one column, *author*, since only that column has same name in both the data sets.

```
proc sql;
select slno, author
    from exam.set1
union corr
select id, author
    from exam.set2;
quit;
```

When the keywords ALL and CORR are used with UNION operator at a time, all the rows (both unique and duplicate) will get displayed which are present in the both the data sets. Only those columns with the same name are displayed in the output. E.g.: The following program shows the operation of an UNION operator with the keywords CORR and ALL. The output of the following query would be all the rows (both unique and duplicate) from both the data sets exam.set1 and exam.set2. Also the output has only one column, *author*, since only that column has same name in both the data sets.

```
proc sql;
select slno, author
    from exam.set1
union corr all
select id, author
    from exam.set2;
quit;
```

71: Explain the significance of OUTER UNION operator.
Answer:

OUTER UNION operator provides the result by combining all the rows (unique and duplicate) from both the data sets. Also it does not overlay the columns.

E.g.: The following program shows the operation of an OUTER UNION operator. The output of the following query would be all the rows from both the data sets exam.set1 and exam.set2. The columns will not be overlaid and it has all the columns from both the data sets - exam.set1 and exam.set2.

```
proc sql;
select *
    from exam.set1
outer union
select *
    from exam.set2;
quit;
```

72: Which operator does not allow the ALL keyword?
Answer:
OUTER UNION operator does not allow the ALL keyword as the OUTER UNION by default includes all the rows from both the data sets in the output.

73: How does the keyword CORR affect the results when used with OUTER UNION operator?
Answer:
The keyword CORR when used with OUTER UNION operator helps to overlay the columns with same name. The result of this operation would be all the rows with same named columns overlaid.

E.g.: The following program shows the operation of an OUTER UNION operator with the keyword CORR. The output of the following query would be all the rows from both the data sets exam.set1 and exam.set2. Also the output has only three columns, *author, slno* and *id*. Since the column name *author* is same in both the data sets, it appears only once in the output.proc sql;
select slno, author

```
    from exam.set1
outer union corr
select id, author
    from exam.set2;
quit;
```

Creating and Managing Tables

74: How do you create an empty table by defining new columns?
Answer:
An empty table can be created with new columns using CREATE
TABLE statement in the PROC SQL query.
E.g.: The following program creates a table exam.set1. Tables are
equivalent to data sets here. set1 is stored in the library *exam*. The
table set1 has 4 columns - *slno, author, marks* and *date*. When this
query is submitted a message is displayed in SAS log, stating that
a table exam.set1 has been created with 0 rows and 4 columns.
proc sql;
create table exam.set1
    (slno int,
    author char(10),
    marks int
    date num format=date9.);
quit;

**75: Which are the various data types supported by the PROC
SQL?**
Answer:
PROC SQL supports 10 different data types - VARCHAR, CHAR,
INT, SMALLINT, NUM, DECIMAL, REAL, DOUBLE, FLOAT and
DATE.

**76: As we all know, SAS supports only two different data types -
numeric and character. So what happens when SAS encounters
additional data types supported by PROC SQL?**
Answer:
When a table is created, PROC SQL converts the other data types
(which SAS does not support) to either character or numeric data
types.
VARCHAR and CHAR get converted to character data type.
INT, SMALLINT, DECIMAL, FLOAT, REAL, DOUBLE, NUM and
DATE get converted to numeric data type.

77: How does PROC SQL affect the column width of data

values?

Answer:

PROC SQL allows you to specify the column width for character data values but not for integer data values.

E.g.: The following program creates a table exam.set1. Here the column, *author*, is assigned a width of 10. Other columns, *slno* and marks are of *int* data type. So they are stored within 8 bytes of storage. So these columns have a default column width of 8 bytes.

```
proc sql;
create table exam.set1
    ( slno int,
    author char(10),
    marks int
    );
quit;
```

78: Which column modifier is not allowed in CREATE TABLE clause?

Answer:

LENGTH= column modifier is not allowed in CREATE TABLE clause.

79: Which PROC SQL statement is used to display the column attributes of a particular table in SAS log?

Answer:

DESCRIBE TABLE statement can be used to display the information about the attributes of column in a table. This is very helpful to understand the structure of a table. Use of this statement writes a CREATE TABLE statement to the SAS log which displays the information about the column attributes.

E.g.: The following program illustrates the usage of DESCRIBE statement. This program writes a CREATE TABLE statement to SAS log, which has all the information about the columns.

```
proc sql;
describe table exam.set1;
quit;
```

80: How does PROC SQL create an empty table which has the same attributes as an existing table?

Answer:

CREATE TABLE statement can be used with a LIKE clause to create an empty table which has the same structure as an existing table i.e. the new table created will have the same column attributes as an existing table.

E.g.: The following program creates a table exam.set2 which has the same structure as exam.set1. The new table will have same column attributes but no data.

proc sql;
create table exam.set2
    like exam.set1;
quit;

81: While creating a table which has a structure just like an existing table, what would you do if some columns need to be removed?

Answer:

While creating a table just like another table it is possible to remove some columns using DROP= option. This can be specified after the new table name in CREATE TABLE statement (between the CREATE TABLE and the LIKE clause) or after the name of the existing table at the end of LIKE clause.

E.g.: The following program creates a table exam.set2 which has the same structure as exam.set1. DROP= option is specified to drop the variable, *marks1*. So the new table, exam.set2 will have all the columns of exam.set1 except *marks1*.

proc sql;
create table exam.set2 (drop= marks1)
    like exam.set1;
quit;

82: How do you create a table from a query result using PROC SQL?

Answer:

To create a table from a query result, CREATE TABLE statement is used with the keyword AS along with query.

E.g.: The following program creates a table exam.set3 by selecting the columns, *slno, marks* and *author* from the tables exam.set1 and exam.set2 where the values of *slno* and *id* match and variable marks has value greater than 80.

proc sql;
create table exam.set3 as
    select slno, marks, author
    from exam.set1, exam.set2
    where set1.slno= set2.id and
    set1. marks>80;
quit;

83: Which statement is used for copying a table?
Answer:
To copy a table, a CREATE TABLE statement can be used with a select query which returns the entire table.

E.g.: The following program creates a table exam.set2 which is a copy of the table exam.set1. Here only two clauses are specified along with CREATE TABLE statement- *select* clause and *from* clause.

proc sql;
create table exam.set2 as
    select *
    from exam.set1;
quit;

84: How do you insert new data to a table using SET clause?
Answer:
SET clause helps to insert data into a table and to specify the new data. A SET clause mentions the column and value in pairs. PROC SQL reads each value and assigns the value to the columns. A separate SET statement is used for each row of data to be inserted.

E.g.: The following program illustrates an example of SET clause. Two rows of data are inserted into the table exam.set1.

```
proc sql;
insert into exam.set1
set slno=245,
    author ='tim',
    marks=80
set slno=3000,
    author='Sam',
    marks=90;
quit;
```

85: How do you use a VALUE clause to insert values for all the columns in a table?

Answer:

When a VALUE clause is used to insert values for all the columns in a table, it is possible to omit the optional list of columns in the INSERT statement. PROC SQL reads the values in the order in which they are specified in the VALUES clause and also inserts values to the columns in the order in which they occur in the table. E.g.: The following program illustrates an example of VALUE clause used to insert the values for all the columns in a table. Two rows of data are inserted into the table exam.set1. exam.set1 consists of three columns – *slno*, *author* and *marks*. The values are inserted into each of these columns.

```
proc sql;
insert into exam.set1
    value( 245,'tim',80)
    value(3000,'Sam',90);
quit;
```

86: How can you use a VALUE clause to insert values for some columns in a table?

Answer:

When a VALUE clause is used to insert values for some columns in a table, it is required to insert the list of column names in the INSERT statement. The values are read in the order in which they are mentioned in the VALUES clause and the values are inserted into the columns in the order in which the columns are specified in the column list.

E.g.: The following program illustrates an example of a VALUE clause used to insert values for some columns in a table. Two rows of data are inserted into the table exam.set1. exam.set1 consists of three columns – *slno, author* and *marks*. The values are inserted into two columns – *slno* and *author*. A missing value is inserted for the third variable which is not present in the list.

```
proc sql;
insert into exam.set1 (slno,author)
    value( 245,'tim')
    value(3000,'Sam',90);
quit;
```

87: How do you insert a row into a table from the query result?
Answer:

It is possible to insert a row into a table from the query result by using an INSERT statement with the clauses used in a query like *select* clause, *from* clause, *order by* etc.

E.g.: The following program illustrates the insertion of a row into a table from the query result. This program selects those rows from exam.set1 whose value of the variable *marks* is greater than 80. These rows are inserted into the table exam.set2.

```
proc sql;
insert into exam.set2
    select slno, author, marks
    from exam.set1
    where marks >80;
quit;
```

88: What is a general integrity constraint?
Answer:

Integrity constraints are set of rules which help to restrict the data values entered for columns. General integrity constraints are those integrity constraints which help in restricting the data values entered for a particular column in a table.

E.g. of General integrity constraints are CHECK, NOT NULL, UNIQUE, PRIMARY KEY.

CHECK - This constraint ensures that a set of values are the only values for a column. This also helps in updating the value of one column with respect to other column for a single row.

NOT NULL - This constraint ensures that the values of a particular column are non-missing.

UNIQUE - This ensures that the values of a particular column are unique.

PRIMARY KEY - A primary key constraint becomes a general integrity constraint if it is not referenced by the foreign key of any other table. This ensures that the values of a particular column are not null and unique.

89: What is a referential integrity constraint?
Answer:
Referential integrity constraints are set of rules which help in linking the data values of column in a table with the column of another table. This is usually created when the primary key constraint is referenced by the foreign key of another table. There are two steps to create a referential integrity constraint - placing a primary key constraint in one table and creating a foreign key constraint in another table which references the primary key of first table.

E.g. of Referential integrity constraint is FOREIGN KEY

FOREIGN KEY is the set of columns of a particular table which reference the values of primary key in any other table. The FOREIGN KEY constraint limits the values of the foreign key of a table as well it affects the values of primary key of the other table.

90: How do you specify the integrity constraint in column specification? Explain with example.
Answer:
Integrity constraints can be specified in the column specifications while creating a table using a CREATE TABLE statement. The integrity constraint can be added in column definition inside the

CREATE TABLE statement.

E.g.: The following program creates a table exam.set1. Here the column, *slno*, is having primary key constraint due to which the values in *slno* will not be null and will be unique. Also another constraint (not null) is placed in the *marks* column due to which the values are never allowed to take null values.

proc sql;
create table exam.set1
   (slno int primary key,
   author char(10),
   marks int not null,
   date num format=date9.);
quit;

91: Explain the CHECK constraint in detail.
Answer:
CHECK constraint enables you to restrict the values of a table based on an expression. When it is mentioned in the CREATE TABLE statement, all the rows of table must conform to the rules mentioned in CHECK expression.

E.g.: The following program creates a table exam.set1. Here the column, *gender*, is having CHECK constraint and NOT NULL constraint. CHECK constraint allows only two values for the column, *gender* - F and M.

proc sql;
create table exam.set1
   (slno int primary key,
   author char(10),
   gender not null check (gender in ('F', 'M')),
   marks int not null
   date num format=date9.);
quit;

92: How do you define the integrity constraints for views?
Answer:
Integrity constraints cannot be defined for views.

93: How do you create the integrity constraint for columns as separate constraint specifications?
Answer:
Integrity constraints can be specified as separate constraint specifications in CREATE TABLE statement. While following this method to create integrity constraints care must be taken to see that the first parameter in the CREATE TABLE statement should be a column specification. After that column specification or constraint specifications can be mentioned in any order. Each specification should be separated by a comma.
E.g.: The following program creates a table exam.set1. Here the constraints are specified separately as constraint specification. A constraint *slno_value* has been defined for the column *slno* which specifies that *slno* is the primary key. A constraint *author_value* has been specified for the column *author* which enforces the NOT NULL constraint.

```
proc sql;
create table exam.set1
     ( slno int ,
     author char(10),
     marks int ,
     date num format=date9.
     constraint slno_value primary key(slno)
     constraint author_value not null(author) );
quit;
```

94: What are the advantages of using a constraint specification rather than creating a constraint using a column specification?
Answer:
Integrity constraints can be created using separate constraint specifications as well as using column specifications in CREATE TABLE statement. The advantages of using separate constraint specifications for creating constraint are that:
   a)   This allows you to create a name for the constraint. While creating a constraint using column specification, SAS automatically creates a name for the constraint.

b) Also, constraints for multiple columns can be created using a single constraint specification.

E.g.: The following program creates a table exam.set1. Here the constraints are specified separately as constraint specifications. Please note that each constraint can be named according to programmer's choice. Also NOT NULL constraint is specified for the columns *author* and *marks* using a single constraint specification.

```
proc sql;
create table exam.set1
    ( slno int ,
    author char(10),
    marks int ,
    date num format=date9.
    constraint slno_value primary key(slno)
    constraint value not null(author, marks) );
quit;
```

The following program creates a table exam.set1. This illustrates the definition of constraint by using column specification. Here SAS automatically assigns the name of the constraint.

```
proc sql;
create table exam.set1
    ( slno int primary key,
    author char(10),
    marks int not null,
    date num format=date9. );
quit;
```

95: Which names should be avoided while defining a name for the constraint?

Answer:

While defining a name for a constraint the following names should be avoided - PRIMARY, FOREIGN, MESSAGE, UNIQUE, DISTINCT, CHECK and NOT NULL.

96: What is the significance of MESSAGE= option in the constraint specification?

Answer:

MESSAGE= option is specified in the constraint specification to write the error message to be displayed in the SAS log when an integrity constraint is violated. The maximum length of the error message is 250.

E.g.: The following program creates a table exam.set1. Here the constraints are specified separately as constraint specification. MESSAGE= option is specified to write the error message to SAS log if the primary key condition is violated.

```
proc sql;
create table exam.set1
    ( slno int ,
    author char(10),
    marks int ,
    date num format=date9.
    constraint slno_value primary key(slno) message= 'ERROR IN
    PRIMARY KEY',
    constraint value not null(author, marks) );
quit;
```

97: Explain the significance of MSGTYPE= option in constraint specification.

Answer:

MSGTYPE= option is used to specify how an error message is displayed in the SAS log when an integrity constraint is violated. There are two values for the option MSGTYPE= : *newline* and *user*. When *newline* is specified as the value for MSGTYPE=, then the error message specified in the MESSAGE= option is displayed in the SAS log along with the default error message for that integrity constraint. When *user* is specified as the value for MSGTYPE=, then only the error message specified in the MESSAGE= option is displayed in the SAS log.

E.g.: The following program creates a table exam.set1. Here the constraints are specified separately as constraint specification.

MESSAGE= option is specified to write the error message to SAS log if the primary key condition is violated. MSGTYPE= option is given the value of *user*. So only the message typed in MESSAGE= option will be displayed in SAS log once an integrity constraint is violated.

```
proc sql;
create table exam.set1
    ( slno int ,
    author char(10),
    marks int ,
    date num format=date9.
    constraint slno_value primary key(slno) message= 'ERROR IN
    PRIMARY KEY' msgtype= user,
    constraint value not null(author, marks) );
quit;
```

98: How does PROC SQL handle the error when UNDO_POLICY= option is set to REQUIRED?
Answer:
UNDO_POLICY= option controls how PROC SQL handles the updated data if there is any error during the updating or inserting of data values. When UNDO_POLICY= option is set to *required*, then if PROC SQL encounters a value in an INSERT statement which violates the integrity constraint, none of the new values in the INSERT statement get added to the table.

E.g.: The following program creates a table exam.set1. Here the column constraints are specified separately. Also a primary key constraint is specified for the column *slno*. A check constraint is specified which enforces an integrity that *marks* has to be always greater than 80. An INSERT statement adds value into the table. Second set of VALUES clause has the value of 60 for the variable *marks*. This violates the integrity constraints.

Since the option UNDO_POLICY= is specified as *required*, none of the values mentioned in the error statement is written to the table. An error message is displayed in the SAS log indicating that add/update failed for the data set exam.set1 because data values do not comply with the integrity constraints.

proc sql undo_policy= required;
create table exam.set1
   (slno int ,
   author char(10),
   marks int ,
   constraint slno_value primary key(slno) ,
   constraint value check (marks ge 80);
insert into exam.set1
   values (25, 'Tim', 80)
   values(30, 'Tom',60);
quit;

99: How does PROC SQL handle the error when UNDO_POLICY= option is set to NONE?

Answer:

UNDO_POLICY= option controls how PROC SQL handles updated data if there is any error during the updating or inserting of data values. When UNDO_POLICY= option is set to *none*, then if PROC SQL encounters a value in an INSERT statement which violates the integrity constraint, that value is not written to the data set but the other values of the INSERT statement which comply with the integrity constraint are written to the data set. E.g.: The following program creates a table exam.set1. Here the column constraints are specified separately. Also a primary key constraint is specified for the column *slno*. A check constraint is specified which enforces an integrity that *marks* has to be always greater than 80. An INSERT statement adds value into the table. Second set of VALUES clause has the value of 60 for the variable *marks*. This violates the integrity constraints.

Since the option UNDO_POLICY= is specified as *none*, the set of values which violate the constraint is not written to the data set; other values are written to the data set. A message is displayed in the SAS log indicating that UNDO_POLICY= option has a value which is different from default (REQUIRED). add/update failed for the data set exam.set1 because data values do not comply with the integrity constraints. The insert failed while rows were added from second VALUE clause. Two rows were inserted into exam.set1 – of these one row was rejected due to error and the other row was inserted successfully.

```
proc sql undo_policy= none;
create table exam.set1
    ( slno int ,
    author char(10),
    marks int ,
    constraint slno_value primary key(slno) ,
    constraint value check (marks ge 80);
insert into exam.set1
    values ( 25, 'Tim', 80)
    values(30, 'Tom',60 );
quit;
```

100: Which statement is used to display only the integrity constraints?
Answer:
DESCRIBE TABLE CONSTRAINT statement is used to display the integrity constraints of a table. Suppose you need to add data to a table and if you are not sure about the integrity constraints, then this statement is of great use.

E.g.: The following program when submitted displays all the integrity constraints specified for the table exam.set1.

```
proc sql;
    describe table constraint exam.set1;
quit;
```

101: Suppose you wish to update the values of a variable for certain rows, how do you do that with PROC SQL?
Answer:
When the values of the variables in a table need to be updated for certain rows, it can be done by using UPDATE statement.

E.g.: The following program illustrates the use of UPDATE statement. Here we wish to add 20 marks to questions which have errors. So 20 has been added to variable, *marks*, for all the questions whose *slno* is between 3000 and 4000.

```
proc sql;
update exam.set1
    set marks= marks+20;
    where slno between 3000 and 4000;
quit;
```

102: Are multiple UPDATE statements allowed in a PROC SQL query?

Answer:

Yes, PROC SQL allows multiple UPDATE statements. But it is not preferred much as it is a cumbersome process to write multiple SET and WHERE expressions. Also the table has to be read as many times as there are UPDATE statements.

E.g.: The following program illustrates the use of multiple UPDATE statements. The purpose of this program is to adjust the marks for those questions which have errors. According to the weightage of the question, different marks need to be added for different questions. So, multiple UPDATE statements are used for updating the data set.

```
proc sql;
update exam.set1
    set marks= marks+5;
    where slno between 100 and 200;
update exam.set1
    set marks= marks+10;
    where slno between 300 and 400;
update exam.set1
    set marks= marks+5;
    where slno between 655 and 700;
update exam.set1
    set marks= marks+20;
    where slno between 450 and 500;
quit;
```

103: How do you use a CASE statement to update a subset of rows?

Answer:

CASE statement is used to update any subset of rows in different ways; conditional processing can be incorporated by using the CASE expression in the *set* clause of an UPDATE statement.

E.g.: The following program illustrates the use of CASE statement to update a subset of rows. The purpose of this program is to adjust the marks for those questions which have errors. According to the weightage of the question, different marks need to be added for different questions. So, different conditions are set. When *marks* value is 10 then it gets multiplied by 5. When it becomes 20 then by 2 and when *marks* is any other value other than 10/20 it remains the same.

```
proc sql;
update exam.set1
    set marks= marks*
case
    when 10 then 5
    when 20 then 2
    else 1
end;
quit;
```

104: Is it possible to use the CASE expression in SELECT clause?

Answer:

Yes, it is possible to use the CASE expression in *select* clause to define a new column.

E.g.: The following program illustrates the use of CASE expression in a *select* clause to define a new column, *levelofexp*. The following expression selects the 6 characters from the values of *jobcategory* and comparison is made based on the extracted value. When the value is 'level1' then *levelofexp* is assigned a value of 'Fresher'. When the value is 'level2' then *levelofexp* is assigned a value of 'Experienced'. When it has any other value, then the new variable has a value 'Unknown'.

```
proc sql;
select name, slno,
case substr(jobcategory,1,6)
     when 'level1' then 'Fresher'
     when ' level2' then 'Experienced'
     else 'Unknown'
end as levelofexp
quit;
```

105: Which statement is used to delete some rows from a table?
Answer:
DELETE statement is used to delete some rows from a table based on subsetting conditions.

E.g.: The following program illustrates the use of DELETE statement to delete certain rows from the table exam.set1. The following program deletes all those rows from exam.set1 where the value of *slno* falls between 550 and 580.

```
proc sql;
delete from exam.set1
where slno between 550 and 580;
quit;
```

106: How do you use an ALTER TABLE statement to add a column to an existing table?
Answer:
ALTER TABLE statement can be used with ADD clause to add a column to an existing table.

E.g.: The following program illustrates the use of ALTER TABLE statement to add a new column *qcat* to the table exam.set11. The program also labels the column as 'QuestionCategory'.

```
proc sql;
alter table exam.set1
add qcat varchar label='QuestionCategory';
quit;
```

107: Is it possible to drop the columns using ALTER TABLE

statement?

Answer:

ALTER TABLE statement can also be used to drop columns of a table. A *drop* clause can be used with ALTER TABLE statement to specify the columns which are to be deleted from the table. Multiple column names must be separated by comma.

E.g.: The following program illustrates the use of ALTER TABLE statement to drop column *qcat* from the table exam.set1.

```
proc sql;
alter table exam.set1
drop qcat;
quit;
```

108: Explain the functionality of MODIFY clause in the ALTER TABLE statement.

Answer:

modify clause can be used along with ALTER TABLE statement to modify one or more existing columns in a table. *modify* clause can be used to change the following parameters of columns - length, format, informat and label.

E.g.: The following program illustrates the use of ALTER TABLE statement to modify the column *qcat* from the table exam.set1. This program adds a new label "CategoryOfQuestions" to the column qcat.

```
proc sql;
alter table exam.set1
modify qcat label = "CategoryOfQuestions";
quit;
```

109: Which are the two parameters of columns which cannot be altered by MODIFY clause?

Answer:

modify clause cannot be used to change the following two parameters.

    a) Data type of a column - *modify* clause cannot be used to convert a character column to numeric and vise versa.

b)   Name of a column - *modify* clause cannot modify the name of the columns.

110: Is it possible to use multiple clauses in a single ALTER TABLE statement?

Answer:

Yes, it is possible to use multiple clauses in a single ALTER TABLE statement to add, drop and modify columns all at once.
E.g.: The following program illustrates the use of ALTER TABLE statement with multiple clauses. This program adds a new column *id* which is of data type *num*. This also modifies the column qcat and labels it as "CategoryOfQuestions". This uses *drop* clause to delete the column *date.*

proc sql;
alter table exam.set1
add id num;
modify qcat label = "CategoryOfQuestions";
drop date;
quit;

111: Which statement is used to delete tables?

Answer:

DROP TABLE statement can be used to delete the tables.
E.g.: The following program illustrates the use of DROP TABLE statement to delete the table exam.set1.

proc sql;
drop table exam.set1;
quit;

Creating and Managing Indexes

112: Explain Simple Index with example.
Answer:
Simple Index is an index based on a single column. Simple index should be given the same name as the column on which it is based. The indexed column can be character or numeric.
E.g.: The following program creates a Simple Index named *slno* based on the column *slno*.
```
proc sql;
create index slno
    on exam.set1(slno);
 quit;
```

113: What is Composite Index?
Answer:
Composite Index is an index based on two or more columns. The indexed columns can be character, numeric or both. Name of a composite index should not be the same as any of the columns or existing indexes.
E.g.: The following program creates a Composite Index named *work* based on the columns *id* and *author*.
```
proc sql;
create index work
    on exam.set1(id, author);
 quit;
```

114: What is Unique Index?
Answer:
Unique Index is an index created to make the values of a column unique. Once a unique index is defined for one or more columns, SAS will reject any changes that would cause more than one row of the table to have same values for specified column or composite group of columns.
E.g.: The following program creates a Simple Index named *slno* based on the column *slno* which is Unique. Use of this index will reject any changes to the table that may be causing the value of *slno* to have non unique values.

proc sql;
create unique index slno
    on exam.set1(slno);
quit;

115: What are the advantages of using an Index?
Answer:
An Index is a file that stores the physical location of values for one or more specified columns in a table. Creating an index for table enables PROC SQL to locate the data more efficiently. There are mainly three advantages of using an index compared to accessing the data sequentially:
a) The use of unique index enables the property of uniqueness to desired columns.
b) Small subsets of data can be accessed more quickly and efficiently.
c) Also the Equijoins can be performed without internal sorts.

116: What are the problems associated with usage of an Index?
Answer:
There are many problems associated with the usage of an Index. They are as follows:
a) Additional CPU Time is required for creation, maintenance and use of an index.
b) Use of index might require additional input / output requests compared to reading a table sequentially.
c) Additional disk space is required to store the index file.
d) Also additional memory for buffers may be required for loading the index pages.

117: Which points are to be considered while creating an index?
Answer:
There are many points to be considered while creating an index:
a) It is not advisable to create indexes for small table as sequential access is faster here.

b) It is necessary to keep the number of indexes to minimum to reduce disk storage and update costs.
c) It is not good practice to create index based on columns that have very small number of distinct values.
d) It is beneficial to create indexes for queries which retrieve relatively small subset of rows.
e) Also it is not advisable to create more than one index that is based on the same column as primary key.

118: Which statement is used to check if an existing table has any indexes?
Answer:
DESCRIBE TABLE statement is used to display a CREATE INDEX statement in the SAS log for each index that is defined for one or more specific tables.
E.g.: The following program displays a CREATE INDEX statement in SAS log for each of the indexes that are defined for one or more specific tables.
proc sql;
describe table exam.set1;
quit;

119: What is the significance of DICTIONARY.INDEXES?
Answer:
DICTIONARY.INDEXES is a special table which contains information about the indexes which are defined for all the tables known to current SAS session. It is one of the many read only tables that are created at PROC SQL initialisation. This also contains information about SAS libraries, macros and other external files that are available in the current SAS session.

120: Which factors are considered by SAS while choosing to use an index rather than reading the data sequentially?
Answer:
Whenever a query is submitted which has a WHERE expression, SAS decides whether to use an index or to read it sequentially. To

decide this, SAS does the following:
   a) It checks all the available indexes.
   b) It estimates the number of rows which would satisfy the WHERE condition.
   c) It then compares the use of index and reading the observations sequentially in terms of resource usage.
   d) It chooses the option whichever utilises the minimum resources.

121: What is the significance of the option MSGLEVEL=?
Answer:
MSGLEVEL= option is used to control how SAS displays information in the log. When a PROC SQL query is submitted, notes, warnings and error messages are written to SAS log by default.

Default value of MSGLEVEL= option is N. When this value is specified, notes, warnings and error messages are written to SAS log when a program is submitted.

When SAS option MSGLEVEL= I is specified, additional messages such as information about the indexes gets displayed in the SAS log. This also displays details related to merging and sorting.
E.g.: The following program displays the content of the table exam.set1. Since the option MSGLEVEL=I has been specified, additional information related to indexes gets displayed in addition to notes, warnings and error messages.

options msglevel=I;
proc sql;
select *
from exam.set1;
quit;

122: Which option is used to direct SAS to use an index or not by overriding the default decision?
Answer:
The IDXWHERE= option is used to override the decision which SAS makes about whether to use or not use an index. It is a SAS

data set option and is specified after the data set name is specified in the *from* clause.

When the option IDXWHERE= YES is specified, it directs SAS to choose the best index available and to ignore the possibility that sequential search might be more resource-efficient.

When the option IDXWHERE= NO is specified, it directs SAS to ignore all the indexes and proceed with sequential search.

E.g.: The following program displays the content of the table exam.set1. Since the option IDXWHERE=NO has been specified, no index is used even if multiple indexes are available. The program proceeds with a sequential search of observations.

```
proc sql;
select *
    from exam.set1(idxwhere =no);
quit;
```

123: Which option allows us to direct SAS to use an index which we specify?

Answer:

The IDXNAME= option is used to direct SAS to use an index which we specify even if SAS had decided to use some other index.

E.g.: The following program displays the content of the table exam.set1. Since the option IDXNAME=slno has been specified, this index is used, even if there are other indexes available.

```
proc sql;
select *
    from exam.set1(idxname =slno);
quit;
```

124: How do you delete an index?
Answer:

The DROP INDEX statement is used to delete an index from a table.

E.g.: The following PROC SQL step uses DROP INDEX statement to drop the index *slno* from the table exam.set1.

```
proc sql;
drop index slno
    from exam.set1;
quit;
```

This page is intentionally left blank

Creating and Managing Views

125: What is PROC SQL VIEW and why is it useful?
Answer:
A PROC SQL VIEW is a stored query expression which reads the data from the underlying files. The underlying files can be SAS data files, DATA step views, other PROC SQL views or DBMS data. PROC SQL VIEWS are virtual tables and do not exist like independent entities.
There are many advantages of using PROC SQL views. They are as follows:

a) This ensures that input data is always the current data as the data is extracted at the execution time.
b) Views save space as a view is very small compared to the data it accesses.
c) It can hide confidential columns from users while enabling the users to update other columns of the same table.
d) It helps users by preventing the continuous submission of queries to omit unwanted columns or rows.
e) It can hide complex joins from users.

126: How do you create a view? Explain with example.
Answer:
A CREATE VIEW statement is used to create a view. A PROC SQL view derives the data from the tables / views mentioned in the *from* clause.
E.g.: The following PROC SQL step uses CREATE VIEW statement to create a view 'exam.seview'. The view exam.seview is a virtual table. The SELECT statement selects all those rows whose value of *slno* matches in both the tables and for which the value of *marks* is greater than 80. When this program is submitted a message gets displayed in the SAS log indicating that the view exam.seview has been defined.
proc sql;
create view exam.seview as
      select set1.slno, id , author
      from exam.set1, exam.set2
where set1.slno=set2.slno

and set1.marks >80 ;
quit;

127: What is the default extension for PROC SQL VIEWS in Windows operating environment?
Answer:
The default extension for PROC SQL VIEWS is *.sas7bvew* in both Windows and Unix operating environments.

128: Is it allowed to use a PROC SQL VIEW in other SAS procedures and data steps?
Answer:
Yes, once a PROC SQL VIEW has been defined, it can be used in other SAS procedures and data steps.
E.g.: The following example illustrates the use of a PROC SQL VIEW in another SAS procedure, PROC PRINT.
The following lines of code create a view 'exam.seview'.
proc sql;
create view exam.seview as
    select set1.slno, id, author
    from exam.set1, exam.set2
    where set1.slno=set2.slno
    and set1.marks >80 ;
quit;

The view is used in the SAS PRINT procedure step.
proc print data =exam.seview;
var slno id author ;
quit;

129: Is it possible to display the definition of a view? If so how?
Answer:
Yes, it is possible to display the definition of a view. This can be done by using DESCRIBE VIEW statement.
E.g.: The following PROC SQL step uses DESCRIBE VIEW statement to display the definition of the view exam.seview in the

SAS log.
proc sql;
describe view exam.seview ;
quit;

130: What happens if the structure of the underlying table changes once a view has been defined?
Answer:
It is not advisable to create views which extract data from the tables whose structure might change. A view is no longer valid when it references a non-existent column.

131: Is it allowed to specify one level name for table in the FROM clause while creating a view?
Answer:
Yes, it is allowed to specify one level name for the table in *from* clause while creating a view if the libref of table in the *from* clause is same as the libref of the view. In case both the libref's are different then you must specify two level names.
E.g.: The following PROC SQL step creates a view 'exam.seview'. The SELECT statement selects all those rows whose value of *slno* matches in both the tables and for which the value of *marks* is greater than 80. When this program is submitted a message gets displayed in the SAS log indicating that the view exam.seview has been defined. Here the tables set1 and set2 are having the libref *exam* which is same as the libref of view *seview*.
proc sql;
create view exam.seview as
    select set1.slno, id, author
    from set1, set2
    where set1.slno=set2.slno
    and set1.marks >80 ;
quit;

132: How do you use an embedded LIBNAME statement?
Answer:

Embedded LIBNAME statement is used to store a libref in a view. It is very advantageous to use embedded LIBNAME statement as it can be used regardless of the situation whether both view and underlying tables are in the same library or not. Also the use of embedded LIBNAME statement eliminates the confusion which arises due to missing libref in the *from* clause.

E.g.: The following PROC SQL step creates a view 'exam.seview'. When the program is submitted, the view exam.seview is created. When the PROC PRINT step executes, the libref result specified in the USING statement becomes active for the duration of view's execution thereby overriding all the previous LIBNAME statements. After the view has been processed, the libref is reassigned.

```
proc sql;
create view exam.seview as
    select set1.slno, id, author
    from result.set1
using libname result 'saslib2';
quit;

proc print data =exam.seview;
run;
```

133: Is it possible to update the underlying data using a PROC SQL VIEW?

Answer:

Yes, it is possible to update the underlying table using a PROC SQL VIEW but only a single table can be updated using a view. The table cannot be linked with other table and cannot contain a subquery. Also it is not possible to update a derived column i.e. a column derived from other columns.

E.g.: The following PROC SQL step creates a view 'exam.seview'. This contains the columns *slno, id, author* and *marks*.

```
proc sql;
create view exam.seview as
    select set1.slno, id, author, marks
```

    from exam.set1
quit;

The following step prints the contents of the view exam.seview.
proc print data =exam.seview;
run;

The view exam.seview is updated. A value of 20 is added to the
marks column for all those rows whose *slno* is between 250 and
260.
proc sql;
update exam.seview
    set marks= marks+20
where slno between 250 and 260;
quit;

134: How do you delete a view?
Answer:
DROP VIEW statement is used to delete a view.
E.g.: The following PROC SQL step deletes exam.seview. When
this program is submitted, a message is written to SAS log
indicating that the view has been deleted.
proc sql;
drop view exam.seview ;
quit;

Processing using PROC SQL

135: How do you restrict the number of input rows while using PROC SQL?

Answer:

INOBS= option is used to restrict the number of input rows while using PROC SQL.

E.g.: In the following program INOBS=5 is specified. Only 5 rows from each of the source tables (exam.set1 and exam.set2) is used. The result of OUTER UNION operator thus has 10 rows.

```
proc sql inobs=5;
    select *
    from exam.set1
        outer union corr
    select *
    from exam.set2;
quit;
```

136: Which option is used to list a column having row number in the output?

Answer:

The NUMBER / NONUMBER option is used to control whether the output from a query will have a column named ROW which displays the row number. The default is NONUMBER.

E.g.: In the following program NUMBER option is specified. As a result the output contains the columns *slno,* id, marks and an additional column row which displays the row number.

```
proc sql inobs=5 number;
    select slno, id, marks
    from exam.set1;
    quit;
```

137: Which option is used along PROC SQL to make the output double spaced?

Answer:

The DOUBLE / NODOUBLE option is used to control the appearance of output i.e. this controls whether the output is double spaced or not. This makes the output easier to read. The default value is NODOUBLE.

E.g.: In the following program DOUBLE option is specified. As a result the output contains the rows which are double spaced. Specifying this option does not affect the appearance of HTML output.

```
proc sql inobs=5 double;
    select slno, id , marks
    from exam.set1;
    quit;
```

138: What is the significance of FLOW= option?
Answer:

The FLOW= option is used to control the appearance of wide character columns while producing list report. The general format of the option is FLOW= N M where N and M specify the limits between which the column width can take a value.

E.g.: In the following program FLOW= option is specified and is set between the limits 10 and 15. This causes the text within each character column to float between 10 and 15. In case there are any values which are greater than the limit, then it is displayed in next row as a part of same observation.

```
proc sql inobs=5 flow= 10 15;
    select slno, id , marks, title
    from exam.set1;
    quit;
```

139: How does FLOW= option affect the HTML output?
Answer:

The FLOW= option does not affect the HTML, PDF or RTF (Rich Text Format) output.

140: Explain the significance of STIMER option.
Answer:

The STIMER option is used to specify that PROC SQL writes timing information for each statement to SAS log instead of writing cumulative value for entire statement. The default value is

NOSTIMER.

E.g.: In the following program STIMER option is specified. When the following PROC SQL step is submitted with STIMER option, the timing information is written in the SAS log for each SELECT statement. Without the STIMER option, timing information is written to SAS log only once for the entire PROC SQL query.

```
proc sql stimer;
    select slno, id , marks, title
    from exam.set1;
    select slno, id , marks, title
    from exam.set2;
    quit;
```

141: How do you check if STIMER option is enabled in your SAS operating environment?

Answer:

The OPTIONS procedure can be used to list the options available in current SAS session. This gives information about the SAS system options which are enabled in the current SAS session. To check if STIMER option is enabled in SAS operating environment, we need to submit the following program.

```
proc options option= stimer value;
run;
```

When the above program is submitted a message is displayed in the SAS log indicating if the STIMER option is enabled.

142: How do you change the PROC SQL options without re-invoking the SQL procedure?

Answer:

The RESET statement can be used to add, delete or change the PROC SQL options without re-invoking the SQL procedure.
E.g.: In the following program, OUTOBS= option is specified to restrict the number of rows in the output to 5. The output of the first SELECT statement will have the columns *slno, id, marks* and *title*. RESET statement is specified to invoke the option NUMBER.

So the output of the next SELECT statement will have the columns *slno, id, marks, title* and *row* (which displays the row numbers). Thus it added the NUMBER option without re-invoking the SQL procedure.

```
proc sql outobs=5;
    select slno, id, marks, title
    from exam.set1;
reset number;
    select slno, id, marks, title
    from exam.set2;
    quit;
```

143: Explain the significance of DICTIONARY.COLUMNS table.

Answer:

The DICTIONARY.COLUMNS table contains information about all the columns in all the tables which are available in current SAS session. The information about a column includes name, length, type, format, informat and label.

E.g.: The following program queries the dictionary table DICTIONARY.COLUMNS to retrieve all the details from those data sets whose libname is *exam*.

```
proc sql;
    select *
    from dictionary.columns
    where libname= 'exam';
    quit;
```

144: Is it possible to update the dictionary table?

Answer:

No, it is not possible to update the dictionary tables as it is limited to read only access. They are created each time they are referenced in SAS program and get updated automatically. Accessing a dictionary table helps in determining the current state of SAS session.

This page is intentionally left blank

Macro Variables

145: What is an automatic macro variable?
Answer:
Automatic variables are those variables created by SAS which contain information about the computing environment like date and time of the session, version of SAS running etc. These variables are created when SAS is invoked and the scope of these variables is global which means that they are always available throughout the SAS session.

E.g.: SYSTIME is an automatic macro variable which has a value equal to the time of invocation of SAS.

146: Name some automatic macro variables which have fixed values set by SAS.
Answer:
Some automatic variables have fixed values which are set when SAS is invoked. Some examples of these types of macro variables are SYSTIME, SYSDATE, SYSDAY, SYSSCP.

a) SYSTIME is an automatic macro variable which has a value equal to the time of invocation of SAS.

b) SYSDATE is an automatic macro variable which has a value equal to the date of invocation of SAS.

c) SYSDAY is an automatic macro variable which has a value equal to day of the week of invocation of SAS.

d) SYSSCP is an automatic macro variable which has a value equal to the abbreviation for the operating system which is used like WIN, HP 300.

e) SYSVER is an automatic macro variable which has a value equal to release of SAS which is used.

147: Explain the macro variable SYSLAST.
Answer:
SYSLAST is an automatic macro variable which has a value equal to the two level name of most recently created data set. The value is stored in capital letters. If there is no data set which is created then it has a value equal to _NULL_.

148: Explain the macro variable SYSPARM.

Answer:

SYSPARM is an automatic macro variable which has value which is the text specified when SAS is invoked.

149: Explain the macro variable SYSERR.

Answer:

SYSERR is an automatic macro variable which has value equal to the return code status set by DATA step or some PROC step to indicate whether the DATA step or PROC step executed successfully.

150: Where are the values of the macro variables stored and where can they be referenced?

Answer:

The values of automatic macro variables are always stored in global symbol table which means that they will be available throughout the SAS session. The values of user defined macro variables are also often stored in global symbol table. They can be defined and referenced anywhere in SAS program except within the data lines of a DATALINES statement.

151: How do you reference a macro variable in a program?

Answer:

A macro variable can be referenced inside a program by placing an ampersand (&) sign before the name of the macro variable.

E.g.: In the following program a new data set exam.set2 is created. A macro variable *value* is referenced in this program by placing an ampersand sign before the variable name. The value of the macro variable is taken from the global symbol table.

```
data exam.set2;
    set exam.set1;
        where marks > &value;
run;
proc print data = exam.set2;
run;
```

152: Is there any particular rule to be followed while referencing a macro variable in a TITLE statement?

Answer:

While referencing a macro variable in a TITLE statement, care must be taken to enclose the text in quotation marks in the TITLE statement.

E.g.: In the following program, the TITLE statement specified has a reference to the macro variable *limit*. So an ampersand is placed before the variable and whole title text is enclosed within double quotes.

```
title "students with marks greater than &limit";
data exam.set2;
    set exam.set1;
        where marks > &value;
run;
proc print data = exam.set2;
run;
```

153: Which statement is used to create a user defined macro variable?

Answer:

A user defined macro variable can be created by using % LET statement. % LET statement enables you to create a macro and assign a value to it.

E.g.: In the following program, a value *Charles* is assigned to the macro variable *author*. Then the macro variable, *author*, is used in the program as well as the TITLE statement.

```
% let author= Charles;
title "work of &author";
data exam.set2;
    set exam.set1;
        where writer = "&author";
run;
proc print data = exam.set2;
run;
```

154: Which all points need to be considered while using %LET statement to create and assign a value to a macro variable?
Answer:
The following points are to be noted while creating and assigning a value to the macro variable using %LET statement:
  a) All the values assigned to the macro variable are stored as character strings.
  b) The case of the value is preserved. So we need to specify the value in exact case which we require.
  c) Quotation marks, if present, are stored as a part of the value.
  d) Mathematical expressions are not evaluated.
  e) Leading blanks as well as trailing blanks are removed from the value before it is assigned to the macro variable.

155: What are the four types of tokens recognized by the word scanner while compiling a SAS program?
Answer:
When a SAS program is submitted, it goes to input stack after which it is sent to the compiler. Between the compiler and input stack, a component called *word scanner* breaks the SAS program into tokens which are the fundamental units.
There are four types of tokens recognised by word scanner. They are as follows:
  a) **Literal token**: This is a string of characters which are enclosed either in single quotes or in double quotes. E.g.: "SAS" or 'SaS'
  b) **Name token**: This is a string of characters which begin with a letter or an underscore and can continue with any combination of letters, numbers and underscores. E.g.: _sas_
  c) **Number token**: This is a string of numerals which can include a period. Date constants, Time constants, Date time constants etc. fall into this category. This also includes real numbers. E.g.: 5
  d) **Special token**: This consists of characters which have

special meaning. E.g.: & , $ etc.

156: Is there any limit on the length of tokens?
Answer:
The maximum length any token can have is 32,767 characters.

157: What is a macro trigger? Give examples.
Answer:
A macro trigger is a certain token sequence which directs the word scanner to send the subsequent code to macro processor. Examples of two macro triggers which are recognised by the word scanner and subsequently sent to the macro processor are as follows:
a) % sign followed by a name token like %limit
b) & sign followed by a name token like &value

158: What are the steps taken by the macro processor when macro triggers are detected?
Answer:
Whenever a macro trigger is detected, the word scanner passes it to macro processor for evaluation. The macro processor examines these tokens, requests if additional tokens are necessary and performs the action indicated.

Whenever macro processor deals with macro variables (which is a type of macro trigger), the processor does one of the following actions:
a) Creates a macro variable and assigns a value to it
b) Changes the value of an existing macro variable
c) Looks the value of macro variable in the symbol table and returns the value to the input stack to use in place of the original reference

159: Explain the SYMBOLGEN option.
Answer:
SYMBOLGEN is an option which is used to specify that the log messages about a macro variable reference are displayed. When

this option SYMBOLGEN is turned ON, SAS displays a message about each of the macro variable reference. This log message contains the macro variable name and value.
E.g.: In the following program the option SYMBOLGEN is turned ON using OPTIONS statement. As a result the SAS log will have messages which indicate the value of referenced macro variable. In the absence of SYMBOLGEN option, i.e. when NOSYMBOLGEN is specified, it is not possible to see or know the value of the macro variable which the compiler receives.

options symbolgen;
% let author= Charles;
title "work of &author";
data exam.set2;
    set exam.set1;
        where writer = "&author";
run;
proc print data = exam.set2;
run;

160: Explain the %PUT statement.
Answer:
% PUT statement is used to write your own messages to SAS log. It can be used to verify the value of macro variables. %PUT statement writes only to SAS log and does not require quotation marks around the text. It can also be used inside or outside the macro definition.
E.g.: When the below statement is submitted the following message is displayed in the SAS log 'The value of the macro variable author is : XXX', XXX being the value of the macro variable.
%put The value of the macro variable author is : &author;

161: Which are the optional arguments used along with %PUT statement?
Answer:
The optional arguments used along with %PUT statement are

ALL, _AUTOMATIC_ and _USER_.

ALL when used along with %PUT statement displays the values of all the macro variables.

AUTOMATIC when used along with %PUT statement displays the values of all the automatic macro variables like SYSDATE, SYSDAY, SYSTIME etc.

USER when used along with %PUT statement displays the values of all the user defined macro variables.

162: What is the significance of using the %STR function?

Answer:

%STR function is a macro quoting function which is used to hide the normal meaning of special tokens and other comparison and logical operators so that they appear as constant text. This enables macro triggers to work properly and also preserves the leading and trailing blanks of an argument.

E.g.: Suppose you wish to create a macro variable *program* and wish to assign the value of 'data exam.set1; set exam.set2; run;'. When the value is assigned to the macro variable, the semicolon present after the data statement may cause SAS to assume that the value of the macro variable *program* ends after the data statement. So the macro variable *program* has a value equal to data exam.set1.

% let program= data exam.set1; set exam.set2; run;

In order to avoid the above problem %STR function is used so that the semicolon present in the value is hid and it is interpreted as normal text.

% let program= %str (data exam.set1; set exam.set2; run;);

When the above line is submitted the macro variable *program* will have a value equal to 'data exam.set1; set exam.set2; run;'.

163: Which function can mask the macro triggers along with capabilities to hide the special tokens?

Answer:

%NRSTR function is a macro quoting function which is used to hide the normal meaning of special tokens and other comparison and logical operators so that they appear as constant text as well as to mask the macro triggers (%, &).

E.g.: Suppose you wish to create a macro variable *author* and wish to assign the value of 'Tom&Harry'.

When the value is assigned to the macro variable, the ampersand present after the initial may cause SAS to interpret it as a macro trigger and an error message may be issued.

% let author = Tom&Harry;

In order to avoid the above problem %NRSTR function is used so that the ampersand present in the value is hid and it is interpreted as normal text.

% let author= %nrstr (Tom&Harry);

When the above line is submitted the macro variable *author* will have a value equal to 'Tom&Harry'.

164: Explain the significance of %BQUOTE function.

Answer:

%BQUOTE function is also a macro quoting function which is used to mask the special characters and mnemonic operators. This %BQUOTE function performs during execution. This function also enables macro triggers to function normally and preserves the leading and trailing blanks in the argument.

E.g.: Suppose you wish to create a macro variable *program* and wish to assign the value of 'student's report' to it.

When the value is assigned to the macro variable, the apostrophe present in the statement may cause an error.

% let program= student's report;

In order to avoid the above problem %BQUOTE function is used so that the apostrophe present in the value is hid and it is interpreted as normal text.

% let program= %bquote(student's report);

When the above line is submitted the macro variable *program* will have a value equal to 'student's report'.

165: Which function is used for changing the case of macro variables?
Answer:
%UPCASE function is used for changing the case of macro variables from lower case to uppercase before substituting the value in the program.
E.g.: In the following program %UPCASE function is used to change the case of the macro variable *author* from lower case to upper case.
options symbolgen;
% let author= Charles;
title "work of &author";
data exam.set2;
    set exam.set1;
        where writer = %upcase("&author");
run;

166: When is the %QUPCASE function preferred over the %UPCASE function?
Answer:
%QUPCASE function is used for changing the case of macro variables from lower case to uppercase before substituting the value in the program. It functions in the same way like %UPCASE function except that it also helps in masking operators and specials characters (including macro triggers).
So in situations that require the macro triggers and special characters to be considered as normal text, %QUPCASE is used instead of %UPCASE function.
E.g.: In the following program %QUPCASE function is used. The %QUPCASE function masks the macro triggers. So the result of this program would be the value '&student'.
options symbolgen;
% let student= Tom;

title "work of &student";
data exam.set2;
    set exam.set1;
        where topper = %qupcase("&student");
run;

167: How does the function %SUBSTR work?
Answer:
%SUBSTR function is used to extract a part of a string from the value of a macro variable.
E.g.: In the following program %SUBSTR function is used to extract a string from the value of the macro variable *date*. Initially *date* is created and assigned a value of 05MAY2012. Then %SUBSTR function is used to extract the three letter word starting at the third position. As a result, the variable, *day*, will have a value equal to MAY.

options symbolgen;
% let student= Tom;
%let date= 05MAY2012;
title "work of &student";
data exam.set2;
    set exam.set1;
        day = %substr(&date, 3, 3);
run;
proc print data =exam.set2;
run;

168: Explain the significance of %SYSFUNC function.
Answer:
%SYSFUNC function is used to execute other SAS functions as a part of macro facility. The main purpose of using %SYSFUNC is to make additional functions and formats available to the macro processor. The use of the %SYSFUNC function enables us to apply the function as the required format to the macro variable in a single step.
E.g.: In the following program %SYSFUNC function is in the

TITLE statement. Here the %SYSFUNC function takes the function *today()* and the format *weekdate.* as arguments. *today()* function returns today's date. The format is specified as *weekdate.* As a result when the program is submitted the title will be work of Tom on Wednesday, May 9 , 2012

```
options symbolgen;
% let student= Tom;
%let date= 05MAY2012;
title "work of &student on %sysfunc(today(), weekdate.)";
data exam.set2;
    set exam.set1;
        day = %substr(&date, 3, 3);
run;
proc print data =exam.set2;
run;
```

169: Explain about SYMPUT routine.
Answer:
SYMPUT routine is used to create a macro variable in a data step and assign a value which is available in the same data step. When a SYMPUT routine is used to create a macro variable in a data step, the variable is created and assigned a value only after the data step is executed.
The general form of using SYMPUT routine is:
call symput(macrovariable to be created, text to be assigned);

E.g.: In the following program, a macro variable, *display*, is created. The value is assigned to the macro variable depending on the value of the variable *marks*. If the value of *marks* is greater than 80, then the macro variable *display* is assigned a value of 'Distinction'. If the value of *marks* is any other value other than 80 then the macro variable, *display*, is assigned a value 'NoDistinction'. The macro variable *display* is referenced in the PROC PRINT step. So, *display* will have the value of either 'Distinction' or 'NoDistinction'.

options symbolgen;
data exam.set2;
    set exam.set1;
        if marks = 80 then call symput('display' , 'Distinction');
        else
        call symput('display' , ' NoDistinction');
run;

proc print data =exam.set2;
title "&display";
run;

170: What are the points to be noted while using a data step variable as second argument of SYMPUT routine?
Answer:
While using a data step variable as a second argument of SYMPUT routine, the following points are to be noted.

a) Name of the data step variable should not be enclosed in quotation marks.
b) A maximum of 32, 767 characters can be assigned to the macro variable.
c) Any blanks (leading or trailing) which are a part of the data step variable are stored as a part of macro variable.
d) Values of numeric variables are automatically converted into character values.

171: Explain the significance of SYMPUTX routine.
Answer:
A SYMPUTX routine functions very similar to SYMPUT routine i.e. it is also used to create a macro variable and assign a value which is available in the data step except that it automatically removes leading and trailing blanks from both the arguments. E.g.: In the following program, a macro variable, *display*, is created. The value is assigned to the macro variable depending on the value of the variable *title*. If the value of *title* is equal to 'technical', then the macro variable *display* is assigned the value of

data step variable 'Technical_Questions'. If the value of *title* is any value other than 'technical' then the macro variable, *display*, is assigned a value of data step variable 'NonTechnical_Questions'. The macro variable *display* is referenced in the PROC PRINT step.

```
options symbolgen;
data exam.set2;
    set exam.set1;
        if title = 'technical' then call symput('display' ,
        Technical_Questions);
    else
        call symputx('display' , NonTechnical_Questions);
run;

proc print data =exam.set2;
title "&display";
run;
```

172: How do you use a data step expression in SYMPUT routine?
Answer:
A data step expression is defined as a combination of functions, data step variables, constants and any operator. The data step expression may resolve to either a numeric or character constant. It can be used in the SYMPUT routine by mentioning it as a second argument without any quotation marks.
E.g.: In the following program, a macro variable, *display*, is created and another expression is used to assign value to it. This expression uses TRIM function to remove the trailing blanks from the variable *Questions_title* and assigns the resulting value to the macro variable *display*.

```
options symbolgen;
data exam.set2;
    set exam.set1;
        call symput('display' ,trim(Questions_title));
run;

proc print data =exam.set2;
```

title "&display";
run;

173: Name some functions which cannot be used along with %SYSFUNC function?

Answer:

Some functions which cannot be used along with %SYSFUNC function are DIF, DIM, HBOUND, INPUT, LBOUND, PUT and SYMGET.

174: Which function is used to obtain the value of a macro variable during execution?

Answer:

SYMGET function can be used to obtain the value of a macro variable during execution.

E.g. In the following program, a macro variable, *writer*, is created and assigned a value 'Henry'. This expression uses SYMGET function to get the value of the macro variable, *writer* and assigns it to the data step variable, *author*.

%let writer= Henry;
data exam.set2;
    author= symget('writer');
run;

175: How do you create a macro variable during the execution of a PROC SQL step?

Answer:

A macro variable can be created during the execution of a PROC SQL step by using INTO clause in the SELECT statement.

E.g.: In the following program, a macro variable, *totalpoints*, is created and assigned a value which is equal to sum of all the values of the variable, *points*. This macro variable which is created during the execution of PROC SQL step is used in the subsequent part of the program which prints the entire data set.

proc sql;
select sum(points) into :totalpoints

```
    from exam.set1;
quit;
%let totalpoints= &totalpoints;
proc print data = exam.set;
title "Points earned &totalpoints";
run;
```

176: Which option is used to specify whether the output of select statement is to be displayed in the output during the creation of a macro variable?

Answer:

The PRINT / NOPRINT option specifies whether the output of SELECT statement needs to be displayed in the output during the creation of a macro variable. Default setting is the PRINT option. E.g.: In the following program, a macro variable, *totalpoints*, is created and assigned a value which is equal to sum of all the values of the variable, *points*. Here the option NOPRINT is specified due to which the output is not displayed even though the macro variable is created.

```
proc sql noprint;
select sum(points) into :totalpoints
    from exam.set1;
quit;
```

177: How do you create a series of macro variables during the execution of a PROC SQL step?

Answer:

A series of macro variables can be created during the execution of a PROC SQL step by using INTO clause. This creates one new macro variable for each row in the result.

E.g.: The following program creates a series of macro variables that contain *slno, type, author* of the first three sets of values in the output. In this example, the macro variable *slno1- slno3* are assigned the values of the data set variable *slno* from first three rows of PROC SQL result. Similarly the macro variables *type1- type3* are assigned the values of the data set variable *type* from first three rows of PROC SQL result and the macro variables *author1-author3* are assigned the values of the data set variable *author* from first three rows of PROC SQL result.

proc sql noprint;
select slno, type, author
    into :slno1 - : slno3,
    into :type1 - : type3,
    into :author1 - : author3
    from exam.set1
    where type = 'technical';
quit;

178: Is it possible to create a macro variable which can hold all the values of a data set variable?

Answer:

Yes, it is possible to create a macro variable which can hold all the values of a certain macro variable.

E.g.: The following program creates a macro variable *writer* which holds all the distinct values of the data set variable *author* separated by blank. The blank is the delimiter used here to separate the distinct values of *author* and is specified in quotation mark.

proc sql noprint;
select distinct author
    into :writer
    separated by ' '
    from exam.set1
quit;

179: Explain the SYMPUTN routine.

Answer:

The SYMPUTN routine enables us to create a macro variable during the execution of a SCL (SAS Component Language) program and assign a numeric value to it.

E.g.: The following line of code creates a macro variable named *marks* and assigns a value equal to 95 to it.

```
call symputn ('marks', 95);
```

Macro Programs

180: How is a macro program defined?
Answer:

A macro program is defined using a %MACRO statement and a %MEND statement.

E.g.: The following program creates a macro program called *lastset* which will print the data set which was created most recently. Please note that SYSLAST is an automatic macro variable which stores the name of data set which was created last.

```
% macro lastset;
    proc print data = &syslast;
    run;
%mend;
```

181: Explain the significance of MCOMPILE NOTE option.
Answer:

MCOMPILENOTE option is used to issue a note to SAS log when a macro has completed the compilation. It can have three values - NONE, NOAUTOCALL and ALL.

When MCOMPILENOTE is having the value NONE, no notes are issued to the log. This is the default value.

When MCOMPILENOTE is having the value NOAUTOCALL, notes are issued to the log for all the completed macro compilation except for the compilation of AUTOCALL macros.

When MCOMPILENOTE is having the value ALL, notes are issued to the log for all completed macro compilations.

E.g.: The following program creates a macro program called *lastset* which will print the data set which was created most recently. The OPTION statement is added which specifies a value of ALL to MCOMPILENOTE due to which a note is issued to the SAS log after compilation.

```
options mcompilenote = all;
% macro lastset;
    proc print data = &syslast;
    run;
%mend;
```

182: How do you call a macro?
Answer:
A macro call is specified by putting a percent sign (%) before the name of the macro. This does not require a semi colon.
E.g.: To execute the macro *lastset* you can submit the following line of program.
%lastset

183: How does a macro execute?
Answer:
When a macro call is made in a program, the word scanner passes it to the macro processor. When the macro processor receives the %macro name, the following actions are performed.
a) It searches the designated catalog for the macro referenced in the program. The default catalog is Work.Sasmacr.
b) It executes the compiled macro language statements defined within the macro.
c) It sends the remaining text to word scanner.
d) It suspends macro execution when it encounters a SAS step boundary.
e) It resumes the execution of the macro after the above SAS step executes.

184: During the macro execution, macro processor communicates with which all components?
Answer:
During the macro execution, macro processor communicates with:
a) **The input stack** - E.g.: The macro processor communicates with the input stack in terms of tokens.
b) **Global and local symbol tables** - E.g.: The macro processor can store the value of a macro variable created using %LET statement.

185: Explain the significance of MPRINT option.
Answer:

MPRINT option is an option which is very helpful in debugging purposes. When MPRINT option is specified, the message, which is sent to SAS compiler after macro execution, is displayed in the SAS log.

E.g.: The following program creates a macro called *lastset* which will print the data set which was created most recently. The OPTIONS statement specifies MPRINT. So the message gets displayed in the SAS log.

```
% macro lastset;
    proc print data = &syslast;
    run;
%mend;

options mprint;
%lastset
```

186: Explain the MLOGIC option.

Answer:

MLOGIC option is the option that displays the actions that were taken during the macro execution in the SAS log. This option is also very helpful for debugging purposes.

When MLOGIC option is in effect, the following information gets displayed in the SAS log:

a) beginning of macro execution
b) result of various operations like arithmetical, logical
c) end of execution

E.g.: The following program creates a macro called lastset which will print the data set which was created most recently. The OPTIONS statement specifies MLOGIC. So the message during the macro execution gets displayed in the SAS log. Here this includes the beginning of execution, name of most recently created data set and end of execution.

```
% macro lastset;
    proc print data = &syslast;
    run;
%mend;
```

options mlogic;
%lastset

187: How do you place comments within a macro definition?
Answer:
Comments can be placed inside macro definition by using macro comment statement. General form of macro comment statement is as follows:
%* comment;
E.g.: The following program creates a macro called *lastset* which will print the data set which was created most recently. Macro comment statement is used to put a comment inside a macro.
% macro lastset;
    %* This is a SAS comment;
    proc print data = &syslast;
    run;
%mend;

188: How do you define a macro having positional parameters?
Answer:
To define a macro having positional parameters, it is required to list the names of macro variables in the %MACRO statement of the macro definition.
E.g.: The following program creates a macro called *printset* which illustrates the example of a macro definition which includes positional parameters. This macro is having the positional parameters - *set1* and *list*.
% macro printset (set1, list);
    proc print data = &set1;
    var &list;
    run;
%mend;

189: How do you call a macro which includes positional parameters?
Answer:

To call a macro which includes positional parameters, precede the name of the macro with a % sign and include the parameters in parenthesis. The values in the brackets should be listed in the same order in which they occur in the macro definition. The values which are listed in the macro call can be text, macro variable references, null values or any macro calls.

E.g.: The following program creates a macro called *printset*. This macro is having the positional parameters - *set* and *list*.

% macro printset (set, list);
    proc print data = &set;
    var &list;
    run;
%mend;

In order to call this macro, the following macro call is used:
% printset (exam.set1, slno author type marks)

When you use the above call the values are assigned to the parameters created in the *printset* macro definition. When the above statement is submitted, *exam.set1* is assigned to the variable *set* and the values *slno author type marks* are assigned to *list*.

190: How do you assign a null value to a positional parameter included in a macro?

Answer:

To assign a null value to a positional parameter included in a macro, it is required to include commas as placeholder for omitted values.

E.g.: The following program creates a macro called *sortset*. This macro is having the positional parameters - *result* and *list*.

% macro sortset (result, list);
    proc sort data = &result;
    by &list;
    run;
%mend;

In order to call this macro, the following macro call is used:
% sortset (, slno author type marks)

When you use the above call a null value is assigned to the positional parameter, *result*. A comma is used to indicate the null value.

191: How do you include keyword parameters in macro definition?
Answer:
To include keyword parameters in macro definition, it is required to list both the name and value of the macro variable in macro definition. Keyword parameters can be listed in any order.
E.g.: The following program uses keyword parameters to create the macro variables *set1* and *list* in the *printset* macro. This example assigns a default value of *exam.set1* to *set1* and *slno marks author type* to *list*.
% macro printset (set1 = exam.set1, list= slno marks author type);
    proc print data = &set1;
    var &list;
    run;
%mend;

192: How do you call a macro with keyword parameters?
Answer:
To call a macro which includes keyword parameters, precede the name of the macro with a % sign and include the parameters in parenthesis. The values in the brackets should be listed in the same order in which they occur in the macro definition. The values which are listed in the macro call can be text, macro variable references, null values or any macro calls.
E.g.: The following program uses keyword parameters to create the macro variables *set1* and *list* in the *sortset* macro. This example assigns a default value of *exam.set1* to *set1* and *type* to *list*.
% macro sortset (set1 = exam.set1, list= type);
    proc sort data = &set1;

```
    by &list;
    run;
%mend;
```

To invoke the macro with the values *exam.set2* for *set1* and *author* for *list*, the following call is issued.
% sortset (set1= exam.set2, list=author)

To invoke the macro with the default values, *exam.set1* for *set1* and *type* for *list*, the following call is issued.
% sortset

193: Is it possible to include a parameter list which contains both positional and keyword parameters in a macro?
Answer:
Yes, it is possible to include a parameter list which contains both positional and keyword parameters in a macro. All the positional parameters must be mentioned before the keyword parameters in the parameter list.
E.g.: The following program uses keyword parameters and positional parameters to create the macro variables set1 and *list* in the *sortset* macro. This macro has both positional parameters and keyword parameters. The default value of *type* is assigned to the macro variable list using the keyword parameter.

```
% macro sortset (set1, list= type);
    proc sort data = &set1;
    by &list;
    run;
%mend;
```

194: Explain the global symbol table.
Answer:
The global symbol table contains automatic macro variables as well as user defined macro variables which are created with the %LET statement in the open code (code that is outside a macro definition)

The global symbol table is created during the initialisation of the SAS session and is deleted at the end of the session.

The macro variables stored in the global symbol table are available anytime during the session and the values can be changed anytime (except for some automatic macro variables).

195: Explain the %GLOBAL statement.
Answer:
% GLOBAL statement is used to create one or more macro variables in the global symbol table. It can be used inside or outside the macro definition.

E.g.: The following program shows the use of %GLOBAL statement to create two global macro variables *set* and *list*. The %LET statement is used to assign values to the global macro variables.

% macro printprog;
    % global set list;
    % let set= exam.set1;
    % let list = slno type author marks;
    proc print data = &set1;
    var &list;
    run;
%mend;

196: How do you delete a macro variable from the global symbol table?
Answer:
% SYMDEL statement can be used to delete a macro variable from the global symbol table.

E.g.: To remove a macro variable, set, from the global symbol table the following command needs to be issued:
%symdel set;

197: What is a local symbol table?
Answer:
A local symbol table is created:

a) when a macro which includes a parameter list is called or
b) when a request is made to create a local variable during macro execution

The local symbol table is deleted when macro finishes execution. The local symbol table contains macro variables which can be referenced anywhere within a macro.

198: What is the function of %LOCAL statement?

Answer:

% LOCAL statement is used to create one or more macro variables in the local symbol table. It can appear only inside a macro definition. This statement does not affect the variables which are already present in the local symbol table.

E.g.: The following program shows the use of %LOCAL statement to create two local macro variables *set* and *list*. The %LET statement is used to assign values to the macro variables.

```
% macro printprog;
    % local set list;
    % let set= exam.set1;
    % let list = slno type author marks;
    proc print data = &set1;
    var &list;
    run;
%mend;
```

199: Is it possible to have a global macro variable and a local macro variable by the same name and different values?

Answer:

Yes, it is possible to have a global macro variable and a local macro variable by the same name but different values since global symbol table and local symbol table exist separately.

E.g.: In the following program, the first %LET statement creates a global macro variable, *set* and assigns a value exam.result to it. The second %LET statement creates a local macro variable, *set* and assigns a value exam.set1 to it.

When the following lines of code are submitted, the first PUT statement prints the value of the local macro variable, which is exam.set1. The second PUT statement prints the value of the global macro variable, which is exam.result.

```
% let set= exam.result;
% macro printprog;
    % local set list;
    % let set= exam.set1;
    % put The value of set inside macro is &set;
    proc print data = &set1;
run;
%mend;
    % put The value of set outside macro is &set;
```

200: Explain the MPRINTNEST option.

Answer:

The MPRINTNEST option is used to specify that the macro nesting information is written to SAS log in the MPRINT output. It is always required to set the MPRINT option along with MPRINTNEST option to specify that the output along with nesting information is written to the SAS log.

E.g.: The following program illustrates a macro nested within a macro. This creates a macro called *lastset* which will print the data set which was created most recently and calls a macro *dispset*. The *dispset* macro has a text message "This is the inner macro".

```
% macro lastset;
    proc print data = &syslast;
    run;
    % macro dispset
    %mend;
% macro dispset;
    This is the inner macro;
%mend;
```

The following lines of code when submitted cause the macro nesting information to be written to SAS log along with the message which is send to SAS compiler after macro execution.

```
options mprint mprintnest;
%lastset
```

HR Questions

Review these typical interview questions and think about how you would answer them. Read the answers listed; you will find best possible answers along with strategies and suggestions.

1: Tell me about your favorite book or newspaper.
Answer:
The interviewer will look at your answer to this question in order to determine your ability to analyze and review critically. Additionally, try to choose something that is on a topic related to your field or that embodies a theme important to your work, and be able to explain how it relates. Stay away from controversial subject matter, such as politics or religion.

2: If you could be rich or famous, which would you choose?
Answer:
This question speaks to your ability to think creatively, but your answer may also give great insight to your character. If you answer rich, your interviewer may interpret that you are self-confident and don't seek approval from others, and that you like to be rewarded for your work. If you choose famous, your interviewer may gather that you like to be well-known and to deal with people, and to have the platform to deliver your message to others. Either way, it's important to back up your answer with sound reasoning.

3: If you could trade places with anyone for a week, who would it be and why?
Answer:
This question is largely designed to test your ability to think on your feet, and to come up with a reasonable answer to an outside the box question. Whoever you choose, explain your answer in a logical manner, and offer specific professional reasons that led you to choose the individual.

4: What would you say if I told you that just from glancing over your resume, I can already see three spelling mistakes?
Answer:
Clearly, your resume should be absolutely spotless - and you should be confident that it is. If your interviewer tries to make you second-guess yourself here, remain calm and poised and assert

with a polite smile that you would be quite surprised as you are positive that your resume is error-free.

5: Tell me about your worldview.

Answer:

This question is designed to offer insight into your personality, so be aware of how the interviewer will interpret your answer. Speak openly and directly, and try to incorporate your own job skills into your outlook on life. For example, discuss your beliefs on the ways that hard work and dedication can always bring success, or in how learning new things is one of life's greatest gifts. It's okay to expand into general life principles here, but try to keep your thoughts related to the professional field as well.

6: What is the biggest mistake someone could make in an interview?

Answer:

The biggest mistake that could be made in an interview is to be caught off guard! Make sure that you don't commit whatever you answer here, and additionally be prepared for all questions. Other common mistakes include asking too early in the hiring process about job benefits, not having questions prepared when the interviewer asks if you have questions, arriving late, dressing casually or sloppily, or showing ignorance of the position.

7: If you won the $50m lottery, what would you do with the money?

Answer:

While a question such as this may seem out of place in a job interview, it's important to display your creative thinking and your ability to think on the spot. It's also helpful if you choose something admirable, yet believable, to do with the money such as donate the first seventy percent to a charitable cause, and divide the remainder among gifts for friends, family, and of course, yourself.

8: Is there ever a time when honesty isn't appropriate in the workplace?

Answer:

This may be a difficult question, but the only time that honesty isn't appropriate in the workplace is perhaps when you're feeling anger or another emotion that is best kept to yourself. If this is the case, explain simply that it is best to put some thoughts aside, and clarify that the process of keeping some thoughts quiet is often enough to smooth over any unsettled emotions, thus eliminating the problem.

9: If you could travel anywhere in the world, where would it be?

Answer:

This question is meant to allow you to be creative – so go ahead and stretch your thoughts to come up with a unique answer. However, be sure to keep your answer professionally-minded. For example, choose somewhere rich with culture or that would expose you to a new experience, rather than going on an expensive cruise through the Bahamas.

10: What would I find in your refrigerator right now?

Answer:

An interviewer may ask a creative question such as this in order to discern your ability to answer unexpected questions calmly, or, to try to gain some insight into your personality. For example, candidates with a refrigerator full of junk food or take-out may be more likely to be under stress or have health issues, while a candidate with a balanced refrigerator full of nutritious staples may be more likely to lead a balanced mental life, as well.

11: If you could play any sport professionally, what would it be and what aspect draws you to it?

Answer:

Even if you don't know much about professional sports, this question might be a great opportunity to highlight some of your greatest professional working skills. For example, you may choose to play professional basketball, because you admire the teamwork and coordination that goes into creating a solid play. Or, you may choose to play professional tennis, because you consider yourself to be a go-getter with a solid work ethic and great dedication to perfecting your craft. Explain your choice simply to the interviewer without elaborating on drawn-out sports metaphors, and be sure to point out specific areas or skills in which you excel.

12: Who were the presidential and vice-presidential candidates in the 2008 elections?
Answer:
This question, plain and simple, is intended as a gauge of your intelligence and awareness. If you miss this question, you may well fail the interview. Offer your response with a polite smile, because you understand that there are some individuals who probably miss this question.

13: Explain *X task* in a few short sentences as you would to a second-grader.
Answer:
An interviewer may ask you to break down a normal job task that you would complete in a manner that a child could understand, in part to test your knowledge of the task's inner workings – but in larger part, to test your ability to explain a process in simple, basic terms. While you and your coworkers may be able to converse using highly technical language, being able to simplify a process is an important skill for any employee to have.

14: If you could compare yourself to any animal, what would it be?
Answer:
Many interviewers ask this question, and it's not to determine which character traits you think you embody – instead, the interviewer wants to see that you can think outside the box, and that you're able to reason your way through any situation. Regardless of what animal you answer, be sure that you provide a

thorough reason for your choice.

15: Who is your hero?
Answer:
Your hero may be your mother or father, an old professor, someone successful in your field, or perhaps even Wonder Woman – but keep your reasoning for your choice professional, and be prepared to offer a logical train of thought. Choose someone who embodies values that are important in your chosen career field, and answer the question with a smile and sense of passion.

16: Who would play you in the movie about your life?
Answer:
As with many creative questions that challenge an interviewee to think outside the box, the answer to this question is not as important as how you answer it. Choose a professional, and relatively non-controversial actor or actress, and then be prepared to offer specific reasoning for your choice, employing important skills or traits you possess.

17: Name five people, alive or dead, that would be at your ideal dinner party.
Answer:
Smile and sound excited at the opportunity to think outside the box when asked this question, even if it seems to come from left field. Choose dynamic, inspiring individuals who you could truly learn from, and explain what each of them would have to offer to the conversation. Don't forget to include yourself, and to talk about what you would bring to the conversation as well!

18: Describe a time when you communicated a difficult or complicated idea to a coworker.
Answer:
Start by explaining the idea briefly to the interviewer, and then give an overview of why it was necessary to break it down further

to the coworker. Finally, explain the idea in succinct steps, so the interviewer can see your communication abilities and skill in simplification.

19: What situations do you find it difficult to communicate in?
Answer:
Even great communicators will often find particular situations that are more difficult to communicate effectively in, so don't be afraid to answer this question honestly. Be sure to explain why the particular

20: What are the key components of good communication?
Answer:
Some of the components of good communication include an environment that is free from distractions, feedback from the listener, and revision or clarification from the speaker when necessary. Refer to basic communication models where necessary, and offer to go through a role-play sample with the interviewer in order to show your skills.

21: Tell me about a time when you solved a problem through communication?
Answer:
Solving problems through communication is key in the business world, so choose a specific situation from your previous job in which you navigated a messy situation by communicating effectively through the conflict. Explain the basis of the situation, as well as the communication steps you took, and end with a discussion of why communicating through the problem was so important to its resolution.

22: Tell me about a time when you had a dispute with another employee. How did you resolve the situation?
Answer:
Make sure to use a specific instance, and explain step-by-step the scenario, what you did to handle it, and how it was finally

resolved. The middle step, how you handled the dispute, is clearly the most definitive – describe the types of communication you used, and how you used compromise to reach a decision. Conflict resolution is an important skill for any employee to have, and is one that interviewers will search for to determine both how likely you are to be involved in disputes, and how likely they are to be forced to become involved in the dispute if one arises.

23: Do you build relationships quickly with people, or take more time to get to know them?
Answer:
Either of these options can display good qualities, so determine which style is more applicable to you. Emphasize the steps you take in relationship-building over the particular style, and summarize briefly why this works best for you.

24: Describe a time when you had to work through office politics to solve a problem.
Answer:
Try to focus on the positives in this question, so that you can use the situation to your advantage. Don't portray your previous employer negatively, and instead use a minimal instance (such as paperwork or a single individual), to highlight how you worked through a specific instance resourcefully. Give examples of communication skills or problem-solving you used in order to achieve a resolution.

25: Tell me about a time when you persuaded others to take on a difficult task?
Answer:
This question is an opportunity to highlight both your leadership and communication skills. While the specific situation itself is important to offer as background, focus on how you were able to persuade the others, and what tactics worked the best.

26: Tell me about a time when you successfully persuaded a

group to accept your proposal.

Answer:

This question is designed to determine your resourcefulness and your communication skills. Explain the ways in which you took into account different perspectives within the group, and created a presentation that would be appealing and convincing to all members. Additionally, you can pump up the proposal itself by offering details about it that show how well-executed it was.

27: Tell me about a time when you had a problem with another person, that, in hindsight, you wished you had handled differently.

Answer:

The key to this question is to show your capabilities of reflection and your learning process. Explain the situation, how you handled it at the time, what the outcome of the situation was, and finally, how you would handle it now. Most importantly, tell the interviewer why you would handle it differently now - did your previous solution create stress on the relationship with the other person, or do you wish that you had stood up more for what you wanted? While you shouldn't elaborate on how poorly you handled the situation before, the most important thing is to show that you've grown and reached a deeper level of understanding as a result of the conflict.

28: Tell me about a time when you negotiated a conflict between other employees.

Answer:

An especially important question for those interviewing for a supervisory role – begin with a specific situation, and explain how you communicated effectively to each individual. For example, did you introduce a compromise? Did you make an executive decision? Or, did you perform as a mediator and encourage the employees to reach a conclusion on their own?

29: Why would your skills be a good match with *X objective* of our company?
Answer:

If you've researched the company before the interview, answering this question should be no problem. Determine several of the company's main objectives, and explain how specific skills that you have are conducive to them. Also, think about ways that your experience and skills can translate to helping the company expand upon these objectives, and to reach further goals. If your old company had a similar objective, give a specific example of how you helped the company to meet it.

30: What do you think this job entails?
Answer:

Make sure you've researched the position well before heading into the interview. Read any and all job descriptions you can find (at best, directly from the employer's website or job posting), and make note of key duties, responsibilities, and experience required. Few things are less impressive to an interviewer than a candidate who has no idea what sort of job they're actually being interviewed for.

31: Is there anything else about the job or company you'd like to know?
Answer:

If you have learned about the company beforehand, this is a great opportunity to show that you put in the effort to study before the interview. Ask questions about the company's mission in relation to current industry trends, and engage the interviewer in interesting, relevant conversation. Additionally, clear up anything else you need to know about the specific position before leaving – so that if the interviewer calls with an offer, you'll be prepared to answer.

32: Are you the best candidate for this position?
Answer:

Yes! Offer specific details about what makes you qualified for this position, and be sure to discuss (and show) your unbridled passion and enthusiasm for the new opportunity, the job, and the company.

33: How did you prepare for this interview?
Answer:
The key part of this question is to make sure that you have prepared! Be sure that you've researched the company, their objectives, and their services prior to the interview, and know as much about the specific position as you possibly can. It's also helpful to learn about the company's history and key players in the current organization.

34: If you were hired here, what would you do on your first day?
Answer:
While many people will answer this question in a boring fashion, going through the standard first day procedures, this question is actually a great chance for you to show the interviewer why you will make a great hire. In addition to things like going through training or orientation, emphasize how much you would enjoy meeting your supervisors and coworkers, or how you would spend a lot of the day asking questions and taking in all of your new surroundings.

35: Have you viewed our company's website?
Answer:
Clearly, you should have viewed the company's website and done some preliminary research on them before coming to the interview. If for some reason you did not, do not say that you did, as the interviewer may reveal you by asking a specific question about it. If you did look at the company's website, this is an appropriate time to bring up something you saw there that was of particular interest to you, or a value that you especially supported.

36: How does *X experience* on your resume relate to this position?

Answer:

Many applicants will have some bit of experience on their resume that does not clearly translate to the specific job in question. However, be prepared to be asked about this type of seemingly-irrelevant experience, and have a response prepared that takes into account similar skill sets or training that the two may share.

37: Why do you want this position?

Answer:

Keep this answer focused positively on aspects of this specific job that will allow you to further your skills, offer new experience, or that will be an opportunity for you to do something that you particularly enjoy. Don't tell the interviewer that you've been looking for a job for a long time, or that the pay is very appealing, or you will appear unmotivated and opportunistic.

38: How is your background relevant to this position?

Answer:

Ideally, this should be obvious from your resume. However, in instances where your experience is more loosely-related to the position, make sure that you've researched the job and company well before the interview. That way, you can intelligently relate the experience and skills that you do have, to similar skills that would be needed in the new position. Explain specifically how your skills will translate, and use words to describe your background such as "preparation" and "learning." Your prospective position should be described as an "opportunity" and a chance for "growth and development."

39: How do you feel about *X mission* of our company?

Answer:

It's important to have researched the company prior to the interview – and if you've done so, this question won't catch you off guard. The best answer is one that is simple, to the point, and shows knowledge of the mission at hand. Offer a few short statements as to why you believe in the mission's importance, and note that you would be interested in the chance to work with a company that supports it.

40: How would you handle a negative coworker?
Answer:
Everyone has to deal with negative coworkers – and the single best way to do so is to remain positive. You may try to build a relationship with the coworker or relate to them in some way, but even if your efforts are met with a cold shoulder, you must retain your positive attitude. Above all, stress that you would never allow a coworker's negativity to impact your own work or productivity.

41: What would you do if you witnessed a coworker surfing the web, reading a book, etc, wasting company time?
Answer:
The interviewer will want to see that you realize how detrimental it is for employees to waste company time, and that it is not something you take lightly. Explain the way you would adhere to company policy, whether that includes talking to the coworker yourself, reporting the behavior straight to a supervisor, or talking to someone in HR.

42: How do you handle competition among yourself and other employees?
Answer:
Healthy competition can be a great thing, and it is best to stay focused on the positive aspects of this here. Don't bring up conflict among yourself and other coworkers, and instead focus on the motivation to keep up with the great work of others, and the ways in which coworkers may be a great support network in helping to push you to new successes.

43: When is it okay to socialize with coworkers?

Answer:
This question has two extreme answers (all the time, or never), and your interviewer, in most cases, will want to see that you fall somewhere in the middle. It's important to establish solid relationships with your coworkers, but never at the expense of getting work done. Ideally, relationship-building can happen with exercises of teamwork and special projects, as well as in the break room.

44: Tell me about a time when a major change was made at your last job, and how you handled it.
Answer:
Provide a set-up for the situation including the old system, what the change was, how it was implemented, and the results of the change, and include how you felt about each step of the way. Be sure that your initial thoughts on the old system are neutral, and that your excitement level grows with each step of the new change, as an interviewer will be pleased to see your adaptability.

45: When delegating tasks, how do you choose which tasks go to which team members?
Answer:
The interviewer is looking to gain insight into your thought process with this question, so be sure to offer thorough reasoning behind your choice. Explain that you delegate tasks based on each individual's personal strengths, or that you look at how many other projects each person is working on at the time, in order to create the best fit possible.

46: Tell me about a time when you had to stand up for something you believed strongly about to coworkers or a supervisor.
Answer:
While it may be difficult to explain a situation of conflict to an interviewer, this is a great opportunity to display your passions and convictions, and your dedication to your beliefs. Explain not

just the situation to the interviewer, but also elaborate on why it was so important to you to stand up for the issue, and how your coworker or supervisor responded to you afterward – were they more respectful? Unreceptive? Open-minded? Apologetic?

47: Tell me about a time when you helped someone finish their work, even though it wasn't "your job."
Answer:
Though you may be frustrated when required to pick up someone else's slack, it's important that you remain positive about lending a hand. The interviewer will be looking to see if you're a team player, and by helping someone else finish a task that he or she couldn't manage alone, you show both your willingness to help the team succeed, and your own competence.

48: What are the challenges of working on a team? How do you handle this?
Answer:
There are many obvious challenges to working on a team, such as handling different perspectives, navigating individual schedules, or accommodating difficult workers. It's best to focus on one challenge, such as individual team members missing deadlines or failing to keep commitments, and then offer a solution that clearly addresses the problem. For example, you could organize weekly status meetings for your team to discuss progress, or assign shorter deadlines in order to keep the long-term deadline on schedule.

49: Do you value diversity in the workplace?
Answer:
Diversity is important in the workplace in order to foster an environment that is accepting, equalizing, and full of different perspectives and backgrounds. Be sure to show your awareness of these issues, and stress the importance of learning from others' experiences.

50: How would you handle a situation in which a coworker was not accepting of someone else's diversity?

Answer:

Explain that it is important to adhere to company policies regarding diversity, and that you would talk to the relevant supervisors or management team. When it is appropriate, it could also be best to talk to the coworker in question about the benefits of alternate perspectives – if you can handle the situation yourself, it's best not to bring resolvable issues to management.

51: Are you rewarded more from working on a team, or accomplishing a task on your own?

Answer:

It's best to show a balance between these two aspects – your employer wants to see that you're comfortable working on your own, and that you can complete tasks efficiently and well without assistance. However, it's also important for your employer to see that you can be a team player, and that you understand the value that multiple perspectives and efforts can bring to a project.

And Finally Good Luck!

INDEX

Advanced SAS Interview Questions

PROC SQL

1: How PROC SQL differs from other PROC statements in SAS?

2: Suppose you are generating a report from the data set exam.questionset1 using PROC SQL. You wish to display the name of the column "author" as "writer" in the report. How do you write the query to modify the report?

3: While generating a report using PROC SQL, how do you sort the rows in descending order of any particular column?

4: What is referred to as "qualifying a column name"?

5: Is there any way to display all the column names from a data set without mentioning the names of the columns?

6: What is the significance of FEEDBACK option?

7: While using PROC SQL, how do you limit the number of rows which is displayed in the output?

8: Which keyword is used to eliminate the rows containing duplicate values while using PROC SQL?

9: Explain BETWEEN-AND operator with example.

10: Explain the significance of CONTAINS operator.

11: How does IN operator function when used with PROC SQL?

12: Which operator is used with PROC SQL to retrieve those rows for which a particular column has missing values?

13: Is there any other operator which can be used in the place of IS MISSING operator?

14: Explain the purpose of using the wild card operator underscore (_) with LIKE operator in PROC SQL.

15: Explain the purpose of using the wild card operator percent (%) with LIKE operator in PROC SQL.

16: Explain the functionality of SOUNDS-LIKE (=*)operator.

17: Is it possible to define a new column after performing a calculation using SELECT clause?

18: How do you reference a column in the WHERE clause, whose value is calculated in the SELECT clause of the same PROC SQL query?

19: How do you specify a label for a column in the PROC SQL query?

20: How do you specify a format for a calculated column in the PROC SQL query?

21: How do you specify a title statement with a PROC SQL query?

22: How do you add a column containing character constant to the output while using PROC SQL query?

23: How is a summary function processed when it has a single argument?

24: Explain what happens when a summary function specifies multiple columns as arguments.

25: How does a PROC SQL process a summary function with a GROUP BY clause?

26: How does a PROC SQL process a summary function without a GROUP BY clause?

27: How does PROC SQL calculate the output when SELECT clause has additional columns listed outside the summary function?

28: How does PROC SQL calculate the output when SELECT clause has no additional columns listed outside the summary function?

29: Which function is used to calculate the total number of rows in a data set or a group?

30: How do you use the COUNT function to calculate the non-missing values for a specific column rather than a data set?

31: How do you use the COUNT function to calculate the unique values for a specific column?

32: What is a subquery?

33: Explain a non correlated multiple value subquery used with conditional operator IN.

34: Explain what happens when a non correlated multiple value subquery is used with outer query having operator ANY.

35: Explain what happens when a non correlated multiple value subquery is used with outer query having operator ALL.

36: Explain operator EXISTS with example.

37: In PROC SQL how do you verify the syntax of the query without executing it?

38: Explain the VALIDATE keyword.

39: What is the main difference between NOEXEC option and VALIDATE keyword?

Horizontal Joins

40: What is a Cartesian product?

41: Explain inner join with examples.

42: What is the maximum number of tables which can be specified in a single inner join?

43: While using inner join, is it possible to specify columns with different names in the join condition?

44: Is column alias allowed while writing a query for inner join of two data sets?

45: How do you specify an alias for a data set in inner join?

46: When does an alias for a data set become essential?

47: Explain the left outer join with example.

48: Explain the right outer join with example.

49: What is a full outer join?

50: Can an inner join be created using an outer join syntax? If so how many tables can be joined at a time?

51: What is the difference between the technique of "data step match merging" and PROC SQL joins?

52: Suppose you wish to merge two data sets by a selected variable, which join will produce the same result as "match merging" when all the values of selected variables match?

53: Explain the COALESCE function.

54: Suppose you wish to merge two data sets by a selected variable, which join will produce the same result as "match merging" when only some of the values of selected variables match?

55: Does PROC SQL allow any other comparison operator other than "equal to" sign?

56: What is an IN-LINE view?

57: Which clause cannot be used with an in-line view?

58: What is the scope of an in-line view?

59: Is it possible to combine an in-line view with other data sets?

60: In how many data sets can the outer join be performed at a time?

61: Is it possible to include multiple data sets in an in-line view? If so how?

Vertical Joins

62: Explain the significance of EXCEPT operator.

63: How are columns overlaid while using an EXCEPT operator in a PROC SQL query?

64: Which keyword can be used with EXCEPT operator to select unique as well as duplicate rows from the first data set?

65: Explain the significance of CORR keyword while used with EXCEPT operator.

66: What happens when both the keywords ALL and CORR are used with EXCEPT operator at a time?

67: Explain the significance of INTERSECT operator.

68: How do the keywords ALL and CORR affect the results when used with INTERSECT operator?

69: Explain the significance of UNION operator.

70: How do the keywords ALL and CORR affect the results when used with UNION operator?

71: Explain the significance of OUTER UNION operator.

72: Which operator does not allow the ALL keyword?

73: How does the keyword CORR affect the results when used with OUTER UNION operator?

Creating and Managing Tables

74: How do you create an empty table by defining new columns?

75: Which are the various data types supported by the PROC SQL?

76: As we all know, SAS supports only two different data types - numeric and character. So what happens when SAS encounters additional data types supported by PROC SQL?

77: How does PROC SQL affect the column width of data values?

78: Which column modifier is not allowed in CREATE TABLE clause?

79: Which PROC SQL statement is used to display the column attributes of a particular table in SAS log?

80: How does PROC SQL create an empty table which has the same attributes as an existing table?

81: While creating a table which has a structure just like an existing table, what would you do if some columns need to be removed?

82: How do you create a table from a query result using PROC SQL?

83: Which statement is used for copying a table?

84: How do you insert new data to a table using SET clause?

85: How do you use a VALUE clause to insert values for all the columns in a table?

86: How can you use a VALUE clause to insert values for some columns in a table?

87: How do you insert a row into a table from the query result?

88: What is a general integrity constraint?

89: What is a referential integrity constraint?

90: How do you specify the integrity constraint in column specification? Explain with example.

91: Explain the CHECK constraint in detail.

92: How do you define the integrity constraints for views?

93: How do you create the integrity constraint for columns as separate constraint specifications?

94: What are the advantages of using a constraint specification rather than creating a constraint using a column specification?

95: Which names should be avoided while defining a name for the constraint?

96: What is the significance of MESSAGE= option in the constraint specification?

97: Explain the significance of MSGTYPE= option in constraint specification.

98: How does PROC SQL handle the error when UNDO_POLICY= option is set to REQUIRED?

99: How does PROC SQL handle the error when UNDO_POLICY= option is set to NONE?

100: Which statement is used to display only the integrity constraints?

101: Suppose you wish to update the values of a variable for certain rows, how do you do that with PROC SQL?

102: Are multiple UPDATE statements allowed in a PROC SQL query?

103: How do you use a CASE statement to update a subset of rows?

104: Is it possible to use the CASE expression in SELECT clause?

105: Which statement is used to delete some rows from a table?

106: How do you use an ALTER TABLE statement to add a column to an existing table?

107: Is it possible to drop the columns using ALTER TABLE statement?

108: Explain the functionality of MODIFY clause in the ALTER TABLE statement.

109: Which are the two parameters of columns which cannot be altered by MODIFY clause?

110: Is it possible to use multiple clauses in a single ALTER TABLE statement?

111: Which statement is used to delete tables?

Creating and Managing Indexes

112: Explain Simple Index with example.

113: What is Composite Index?

114: What is Unique Index?

115: What are the advantages of using an Index?

116: What are the problems associated with usage of an Index?

117: Which points are to be considered while creating an index?

118: Which statement is used to check if an existing table has any indexes?

119: What is the significance of DICTIONARY.INDEXES?

120: Which factors are considered by SAS while choosing to use an index rather than reading the data sequentially?

121: What is the significance of the option MSGLEVEL=?

122: Which option is used to direct SAS to use an index or not by overriding the default decision?

123: Which option allows us to direct SAS to use an index which we specify?

124: How do you delete an index?

Creating and Managing Views

125: What is PROC SQL VIEW and why is it useful?

126: How do you create a view? Explain with example.

127: What is the default extension for PROC SQL VIEWS in Windows operating environment?

128: Is it allowed to use a PROC SQL VIEW in other SAS procedures and data steps?

129: Is it possible to display the definition of a view? If so how?

130: What happens if the structure of the underlying table changes once a view has been defined?

131: Is it allowed to specify one level name for table in the FROM clause while creating a view?

132: How do you use an embedded LIBNAME statement?

133: Is it possible to update the underlying data using a PROC SQL VIEW?

134: How do you delete a view?

Processing using PROC SQL

135: How do you restrict the number of input rows while using PROC SQL?

136: Which option is used to list a column having row number in the output?

137: Which option is used along PROC SQL to make the output double spaced?

138: What is the significance of FLOW= option?

139: How does FLOW= option affect the HTML output?

140: Explain the significance of STIMER option.

141: How do you check if STIMER option is enabled in your SAS operating environment?

142: How do you change the PROC SQL options without re-invoking the SQL procedure?

143: Explain the significance of DICTIONARY.COLUMNS table.

144: Is it possible to update the dictionary table?

Macro Variables

145: What is an automatic macro variable?

146: Name some automatic macro variables which have fixed values set by SAS.

147: Explain the macro variable SYSLAST.

148: Explain the macro variable SYSPARM.

149: Explain the macro variable SYSERR.

150: Where are the values of the macro variables stored and where can they be referenced?

151: How do you reference a macro variable in a program?

152: Is there any particular rule to be followed while referencing a macro variable in a TITLE statement?

153: Which statement is used to create a user defined macro variable?

154: Which all points need to be considered while using %LET statement to create and assign a value to a macro variable?

155: What are the four types of tokens recognized by the word scanner while compiling a SAS program?

156: Is there any limit on the length of tokens?

157: What is a macro trigger? Give examples.

158: What are the steps taken by the macro processor when macro triggers are detected?

159: Explain the SYMBOLGEN option.

160: Explain the %PUT statement.

161: Which are the optional arguments used along with %PUT statement?

162: What is the significance of using the %STR function?

163: Which function can mask the macro triggers along with capabilities to hide the special tokens?

164: Explain the significance of %BQUOTE function.

165: Which function is used for changing the case of macro variables?

166: When is the %QUPCASE function preferred over the %UPCASE function?

167: How does the function %SUBSTR work?

168: Explain the significance of %SYSFUNC function.

169: Explain about SYMPUT routine.

170: What are the points to be noted while using a data step variable as second argument of SYMPUT routine?

171: Explain the significance of SYMPUTX routine.

172: How do you use a data step expression in SYMPUT routine?

173: Name some functions which cannot be used along with %SYSFUNC function.

174: Which function is used to obtain the value of a macro variable during execution?

175: How do you create a macro variable during the execution of a PROC SQL step?

176: Which option is used to specify whether the output of select statement is to be displayed in the output during the creation of a macro variable?

177: How do you create a series of macro variables during the execution of a PROC SQL step?

178: Is it possible to create a macro variable which can hold all the values of a data set variable?

179: Explain the SYMPUTN routine.

Macro Programs

180: How is a macro program defined?

181: Explain the significance of MCOMPILE NOTE option.

182: How do you call a macro?

183: How does a macro execute?

184: During the macro execution, macro processor communicates with which all components?

185: Explain the significance of MPRINT option.

186: Explain the MLOGIC option.

187: How do you place comments within a macro definition?

188: How do you define a macro having positional parameters?

189: How do you call a macro which includes positional parameters?

190: How do you assign a null value to a positional parameter included in a macro?

191: How do you include keyword parameters in macro definition?

192: How do you call a macro with keyword parameters?

193: Is it possible to include a parameter list which contains both positional and keyword parameters in a macro?

194: Explain the global symbol table.

195: Explain the %GLOBAL statement.

196: How do you delete a macro variable from the global symbol table?
197: What is a local symbol table?
198: What is the function of %LOCAL statement?
199: Is it possible to have a global macro variable and a local macro variable by the same name and different values?
200: Explain the MPRINTNEST option.

HR Questions

1: Tell me about your favorite book or newspaper.

2 If you could be rich or famous, which would you choose?

3: If you could trade places with anyone for a week, who would it be and why?

4: What would you say if I told you that just from glancing over your resume, I can already see three spelling mistakes?

5: Tell me about your worldview.

6: What is the biggest mistake someone could make in an interview?

7: If you won the $50m lottery, what would you do with the money?

8: Is there ever a time when honesty isn't appropriate in the workplace?

9: If you could travel anywhere in the world, where would it be?

10: What would I find in your refrigerator right now?

11: If you could play any sport professionally, what would it be and what aspect draws you to it?

12: Who were the presidential and vice-presidential candidates in the 2008 elections?

13: Explain X *task* in a few short sentences as you would to a second-grader.

14: If you could compare yourself to any animal, what would it be?

15: Who is your hero?

16: Who would play you in the movie about your life?

17: Name five people, alive or dead, that would be at your ideal dinner party.

18: Describe a time when you communicated a difficult or complicated idea to a coworker.

19: What situations do you find it difficult to communicate in?

20: What are the key components of good communication?

21 Tell me about a time when you solved a problem through communication?

22: Tell me about a time when you had a dispute with another employee. How did you resolve the situation?

23: Do you build relationships quickly with people, or take more time to get to know them?

24: Describe a time when you had to work through office politics to solve a problem.

25: Tell me about a time when you persuaded others to take on a difficult task?

26: Tell me about a time when you successfully persuaded a group to accept your proposal.

27: Tell me about a time when you had a problem with another person, that, in hindsight, you wished you had handled differently.

28: Tell me about a time when you negotiated a conflict between other employees.

29: Why would your skills be a good match with X *objective* of our company?

30: What do you think this job entails?

31: Is there anything else about the job or company you'd like to know?

32: Are you the best candidate for this position?

33: How did you prepare for this interview?

34: If you were hired here, what would you do on your first day?

35: Have you viewed our company's website?

36: How does X *experience* on your resume relate to this position?

37: Why do you want this position?

38: How is your background relevant to this position?

39: How do you feel about X *mission* of our company?

40: How would you handle a negative coworker?

41: What would you do if you witnessed a coworker surfing the web, reading a book, etc, wasting company time?

42: How do you handle competition among yourself and other employees?

43: When is it okay to socialize with coworkers?

44: Tell me about a time when a major change was made at your last job, and how you handled it.

45: When delegating tasks, how do you choose which tasks go to which team members?

46: Tell me about a time when you had to stand up for something you believed strongly about to coworkers or a supervisor.

47: Tell me about a time when you helped someone finish their work, even though it wasn't "your job."

48: What are the challenges of working on a team? How do you handle this?

49: Do you value diversity in the workplace?

50: How would you handle a situation in which a coworker was not accepting of someone else's diversity?

51: Are you rewarded more from working on a team, or accomplishing a task on your own?

Some of the following titles might also be handy:

1. .NET Interview Questions You'll Most Likely Be Asked
2. 200 Interview Questions You'll Most Likely Be Asked
3. Access VBA Programming Interview Questions You'll Most Likely Be Asked
4. Adobe ColdFusion Interview Questions You'll Most Likely Be Asked
5. Advanced JAVA Interview Questions You'll Most Likely Be Asked
6. Advanced SAS Interview Questions You'll Most Likely Be Asked
7. AJAX Interview Questions You'll Most Likely Be Asked
8. Algorithms Interview Questions You'll Most Likely Be Asked
9. Android Development Interview Questions You'll Most Likely Be Asked
10. Ant & Maven Interview Questions You'll Most Likely Be Asked
11. Apache Web Server Interview Questions You'll Most Likely Be Asked
12. ASP.NET Interview Questions You'll Most Likely Be Asked
13. Automated Software Testing Interview Questions You'll Most Likely Be Asked
14. Base SAS Interview Questions You'll Most Likely Be Asked
15. BEA WebLogic Server Interview Questions You'll Most Likely Be Asked
16. C & C++ Interview Questions You'll Most Likely Be Asked
17. C# Interview Questions You'll Most Likely Be Asked
18. C++ Internals Interview Questions You'll Most Likely Be Asked
19. CCNA Interview Questions You'll Most Likely Be Asked
20. Cloud Computing Interview Questions You'll Most Likely Be Asked
21. Computer Architecture Interview Questions You'll Most Likely Be Asked
22. Computer Networks Interview Questions You'll Most Likely Be Asked
23. Core JAVA Interview Questions You'll Most Likely Be Asked
24. Data Structures & Algorithms Interview Questions You'll Most Likely Be Asked
25. Data WareHousing Interview Questions You'll Most Likely Be Asked
26. EJB 3.0 Interview Questions You'll Most Likely Be Asked
27. Entity Framework Interview Questions You'll Most Likely Be Asked
28. Fedora & RHEL Interview Questions You'll Most Likely Be Asked
29. GNU Development Interview Questions You'll Most Likely Be Asked
30. Hibernate, Spring & Struts Interview Questions You'll Most Likely Be Asked
31. HTML, XHTML and CSS Interview Questions You'll Most Likely Be Asked
32. HTML5 Interview Questions You'll Most Likely Be Asked
33. IBM WebSphere Application Server Interview Questions You'll Most Likely Be Asked
34. iOS SDK Interview Questions You'll Most Likely Be Asked
35. Java / J2EE Design Patterns Interview Questions You'll Most Likely Be Asked
36. Java / J2EE Interview Questions You'll Most Likely Be Asked
37. Java Messaging Service Interview Questions You'll Most Likely Be Asked
38. JavaScript Interview Questions You'll Most Likely Be Asked
39. JavaServer Faces Interview Questions You'll Most Likely Be Asked
40. JDBC Interview Questions You'll Most Likely Be Asked
41. jQuery Interview Questions You'll Most Likely Be Asked

For complete list visit
www.vibrantpublishers.com

NOTES